TYLER D. SMITH

SEARCHING
FOR
SEVEN

The Journey of Seeking God
Seven Days a Week

CLAY BRIDGES
PRESS

Searching for Seven
The Journey of Seeking God Seven Days a Week

Copyright © 2020 by Tyler D. Smith

Published by Clay Bridges in Houston, TX
www.ClayBridgesPress.com

ISBN: 978-1-939815-60-6
eISBN: 978-1-939815-96-5

Contents

*Thank you to my wife, Katelyn, for your love and support.
Thank you to my parents and sister for demonstrating
what it's like to follow Jesus every day.*

*Thank you to Lincoln Christian University and
all the people there for helping to shape who I am. Thank you
also to all the students and players I've had over the years:
you are my inspiration and encouragement.*

*And of course, thank you to my God for giving me
more grace and love than I'll ever deserve.*

Chapter One

The Search Begins

One basketball game changed my entire life.

It wasn't even a championship game or a game that anybody else would even remember. When it happened, I had no idea what it would mean for my future. It took many years before I realized how much it altered my life. Have you had something happen that seemed inconsequential at the time turn out to be a game-changer when you looked back years later?

I was just a sophomore in high school at the time, playing basketball where the game was invented—in the great state of Indiana. I was what you call a "late bloomer." I was skinny, shy, and not very confident. I had always dreamed of playing varsity basketball, but things weren't looking too promising at the time for me to accomplish that goal.

I was on the JV team and wasn't playing very much because our school had a lot of talent in the grades above me and quite a bit of talent coming up behind me. All it took was three kids getting kicked off the team, and I had my chance. I would've preferred a different way to the promised land of starting on the JV team, but what are you going to do?

Unfortunately, I wasn't taking advantage of my new opportunity. In fact, I was probably making things worse. And then came the one night that changed it all.

I was trying to guard the other team's best player. *Try* is the key word. I couldn't hit the broad side of a barn on offense and couldn't guard anybody on defense. Not a great combination. The coach pulled me out of the game, started yelling at me, and because I was one of those 15-year-olds who knew everything, I talked back to the coach. For some reason, he didn't agree with me, so he yelled some more.

I sat down at the end of the bench and thought, "My basketball career is not looking great." I couldn't have predicted what happened next. Not even two minutes later, the coach came back over to me and put me back in the game. I thought, "Seriously? You want me back in the game? I'm playing like trash, and I just mouthed off to you. Were you trying to point to somebody else?"

Adrenaline can be a wonderful thing. My blood was boiling from what had just happened. I was mad at the coach for yelling at me. I was mad we were losing. I was mad at myself for playing so poorly. As it turns out, this emotional intensity was exactly what I needed.

I ended up playing the best half of basketball I had ever played up until then. From that point on and for the rest of the season, I had a newfound confidence. I started playing up to my capabilities. I started playing with aggression and confidence. I played so well that by the end of my sophomore year, I ended up dressing for varsity. I played varsity my junior and senior years and had a chance to play in college.

But this story is not about my basketball success. This book is not about my accomplishments. It's about what God has taught me along the way in this journey called life as I search for Him.

When I finished high school, my plan was to go into sports broadcasting and major in mass communication. I went to Indiana State my first year but felt like God was calling me elsewhere. I was really missing basketball, and Lincoln Christian University had some interest in me as a student-athlete. I decided to visit and try out for the team. Lincoln had a communication studies degree program, so I could play ball, be surrounded by other Christians, and continue with my same major. I remember telling God, "Okay, God. If I make this basketball team, I'm going to take that as a sign that I should transfer." That's not always the best way to go about things, but it worked out in this case. I made the team and began the process of transferring schools.

After one year at Lincoln, I got a phone call from a local church asking if I would consider starting a youth group for them. I kid you not, my first thought was: "Yes! I don't have to work in a factory this summer!" I had no intention of youth ministry as a career, but God had other plans. This new youth group job was supposed to just be a summer thing, but I've been in youth ministry ever since.

Let me break it down like this: The only reason I got into youth ministry was because I went to Lincoln. The only reason I went to that college was because of basketball. And the only reason I was good enough in basketball was because of what started one night as a 15-year-old JV basketball player. I still tell people to this day: if it wasn't for that one game, I have no idea where I would be today. No basketball = No Christian college. No Christian college = No youth ministry career.

Maybe the best part of this story is what God taught me years later. Looking back, I realized that what my coach did that night is exactly what God does in our lives. When we've screwed up in life, when things aren't going as planned, when we "talk back" to Him like a bunch of know-it-alls, He doesn't just leave us on the bench. He comes right back over to us and puts us back in the game.

Scripture is filled with people who screwed up countless times. Some of them were the closest allies of Jesus who walked with Him daily. Did He ever give up on them? Never. It would have been very easy for Him to tell His disciples or someone caught in sin, "You've screwed up one too many times. Stay on the bench. You're done."

But we know that's not how the story goes. So why do we pretend like that's how our story goes? Do you think you can't be forgiven? The Apostle Paul says hello. Do you think you've screwed up too many times to be used by God? Peter would like a word.

The truth is that God wants to use you and me in spite of our past. He knows what we're capable of. And if we allow Him to use us, there's no telling what path He will take us in the future. Following Jesus isn't about one big event in our lives. It's not about going to worship once a week. It's about the journey. It's about leaning into what He's teaching you along the way, even if you don't realize what He was doing until years later.

I want to live my life Searching for Seven. I want to be searching for completeness. I want to live out my faith seven days a week. I want to be looking for my Creator through all life's adventures.

A lot of people say, "I'd believe in God if He'd just show Himself to me," but they do nothing to seek Him. How will we find Him if we're not looking? It's hard to find what we're not actively searching for. So, let the search begin.

It's time to get back in the game.

Chapter Two

When in Doubt, Serve

I have a scooter in the shed outside my house. You don't know what living is until you're racing around at an incredible 35 miles an hour through town with the wind at your back. Owning a scooter also gives you the perfect excuse to quote *Dumb and Dumber* lines all day.

When I ride my scooter regularly, it works great. She fires right up and gets about a thousand miles per gallon. The problem is, I have many other priorities in life, and she often gets neglected. If I don't take her out once in a while, she gets a little restless, which is also good dating advice.

After not being used for a while, my scooter starts to develop problems. Eventually, it stops working altogether. The reason? It wasn't made to sit in a shed for months at a time. We are wired in a similar way when it comes to our faith.

We are "created in Christ Jesus to do good works" (Eph. 2:10). We weren't created to just sit back and do nothing. We weren't created to only follow our own desires. We were created to do good works, which He prepared in advance for us to do. We were created to serve and bring glory to God while doing good works.

So when we aren't putting action to our faith, it's like we're wasting away on the inside, just like the scooter in the shed. When something isn't being used for what it was created to do, the rotting away begins. It's hard to feel purpose in life if you're rotting away instead of doing what you were created to do. In contrast to that, we are most alive when we're using our gifts.

Should a Christian ever be bored or apathetic toward life? Think about it.

If we have a life-changing book, a life-changing message, and a life-changing mission, why do we so often pretend we don't have much of a life? Even if you don't like your job, what if you treated it like your personal mission field? Or if you feel like life hasn't given you much, what if you treated your life like it was something to give away?

In most cases, I believe that our boredom or apathy is self-inflicted. If we're not living with a purpose, it's completely on us to change that. I can promise you the disciples were never bored. I can promise you the early church members were never apathetic toward life. They knew that life is short and that Christianity is supposed to be a life full of risk and adventure.

I believe every Christian should have their own ministry. Some will have a pulpit, and others won't. But each and every believer in Jesus Christ should have their own mission and their own ministry to carry out. What are your gifts? What are you passionate about? Who needs to hear about Jesus? What problems in the world today upset you? Answering these questions will give each of us a great start.

Maybe you feel like God is distant in your life. My best advice is to start serving more. We're never more like Jesus than when we are loving and serving other people. If we want to experience Jesus more, we need to go where His children are and join Him in His mission. I've never heard someone come home from a mission trip and say, "I just don't know where God is." Or after someone serves at a soup kitchen or homeless shelter, do you ever hear them saying that God is distant?

Maybe you feel your marriage is stagnant. Start serving together and see what happens. As Francis Chan says, "Being in war together is what keeps us from being at war with each other."[1] He's talking about serving others as a couple and being on mission with Christ instead of only thinking about our own desires.

Recently, I was asked how to give advice to someone who is depressed. I had a similar answer for that person. Put more action to your faith and start serving as much as possible. Don't get me wrong, I don't pretend to have answers for something as serious as depression. But I truly believe involving yourself more in serving others would be a step in the right direction. I feel my life has more meaning, purpose, and value when I'm serving someone else rather than myself.

If you have a suicidal friend, invite them to serve with you somewhere. You never know what that could do for their life if they are yearning for purpose. If someone is skeptical about going to church, invite them to serve with the church first. Maybe they'll see it's about more than a building and then be more open to the whole idea.

The world views success in different ways—money, fame, popularity, power, and the like. Success in the eyes of Jesus is all about serving others (Mark 10:43). He came and washed the nasty feet of the disciples and then went to a cross to show what serving others truly looked like.

I still remember my "dorm-floor initiation" at Lincoln Christian University like it was yesterday. The upperclassmen told us they were going to initiate the new students, and we all started wondering what they were going to make us do. Instead of making us do anything, the upperclassmen washed our feet. At the time, I thought it was a little weird. I'm not usually a fan of someone else touching my feet. As time has passed, however, that experience has left a huge impression on my life. Christ came to serve, and we were created in Him to serve. Not only does it help the people we're serving, but it also gives purpose and meaning to our own souls.

Can you imagine the example you could set as a high school senior if you became a mentor for a freshman instead of hazing or ignoring them? Can you imagine the example you could set as the company boss if you served your fellow employees instead of just using them for your own personal gain? Jesus flipped the world upside down with His view of serving. Maybe it's time we joined Him.

As it says in 1 Corinthians 15:58, "Always give yourselves fully to the work of the Lord, because you know that your labor in the Lord is not in vain."

Whenever we serve somebody, we're doing the work of the Lord. You may not always see the fruit of your labor. You may not feel like you're making a difference. But our labor in the Lord is not in vain. Pick a random day from years ago and try to remember what you had to eat that day. I don't remember what I had to eat on September 5, 2004, but whatever I ate that day gave me life, right? Our acts of service may not always be remembered years later, but they can give life to others in the moment. That should keep us moving forward.

Martin Luther King Jr. said, "Everybody can be great, because anybody can serve."[2] So, go be great! Life is too short to remain apathetic. Jesus is too incredible to remain bored with the mission. Be the church. Be His hands and feet. There is no such thing as an "unsent" Christian. When in doubt, serve.

Our faith was never meant to sit in a shed.

Chapter Three

Faith

I love the story of a man named Charles Blondin. Blondin was a famous tightrope walker, and in September 1860 he became the first person to tightrope across Niagara Falls. He was almost 200 feet in the air, and he walked over 11,000 feet across Niagara Gorge. A large crowd gathered, and they were astonished at what they saw. They cheered loudly, and they were excited to witness this incredible feat.

Blondin didn't just walk across the tightrope one time. He went back and forth several times, and each time he would add something different to his act. One time, he did it blindfolded. One time, he did it on a bicycle. One time, he had a wheelbarrow full of potatoes that he was pushing across the tightrope.

Then, at one point, Blondin addressed the audience and asked, "Do you believe I can carry a person across in this wheelbarrow?" The crowd let out an emphatic roar of approval. One man shouted, "Yes! You're the greatest tightrope walker in the world. We believe you can do it!"

Then Blondin said, "Okay, great! I need a volunteer! Who wants to get in the wheelbarrow?" And there was silence.

Not one person volunteered to get in. They all loved watching the show. And they all had evidence that this man was a professional. But not one person had the trust to put their life in his hands.

That story can teach us a lot about faith. At times, we love to see God at work. We believe He can do great things. We even have evidence of His work. But it's a different story for us to put our lives completely in His hands. It's one thing to believe. It's another thing to put action to what we believe.

I think it would help if we truly knew what faith was all about. Is it really blind belief? *Merriam-Webster.com Dictionary* defines *faith* as "firm belief in something for which there is no proof." Is that the kind of faith we have, though? When you think of faith, do you think of it the way *Merriam-Webster* defines it? Or, do you think of faith the way the writer of Hebrews defines it?

In Hebrews 11:1, we have a definition of the word *faith*. And I want you to focus on some key words in this verse: "To have faith is to be sure of the things we hope for, to be certain of the things we cannot see" (GNT). Even if we can't see God, this verse makes it clear that we still have an assurance of His existence. The dictionary may say *faith* means having no proof, but God says we can be sure and certain of what we hope for and what we don't see.

Christian apologist Frank Turek makes the case that there's a difference between faith "that" something exists and faith "in" something that exists. For example, in the book of James, it says, "Even the demons believe" *that* God exists, but they don't put their trust *in* Him. They know intellectually that He exists but they still choose not to follow Him. More often than not, when the Bible talks about faith, it's talking more about faith *in* God rather than just an intellectual belief that God exists. We have evidence of God's existence, but then it's up to us to put our faith *in* Him with our lives. I don't believe I have faith without evidence. The evidence is one reason I have faith.

Here's something interesting to consider. Based on the Bible's definition of *faith,* can I have faith in something like a sports team? Can I have faith that my Cubbies will win the World Series? Based on the Bible's definition of *faith*, the answer is no. We shouldn't confuse faith with hope. I hope the Cubs will win another World Series, but can I be absolutely sure and certain? No. And you may ask, why is that important?

Well, imagine that I was talking with a friend, and I told my friend, "I have faith in the Cubs this year. They've got a great team; I have faith in my team to win it all." Then, let's say the Cubs don't win the World Series. And the next time I talk to that same friend, I say, "I have faith that God exists." Do you see why that could be a problem? My friend could easily think to himself: "Oh, you have faith in God? Kind of like you had faith in the Cubs this year too, huh?" Too many Christians treat faith like it's the worldly definition kind. They treat faith like it's actually hope. But a blind faith is not what we have. Our faith is based on being sure and certain.

Consider this: If somebody were to ask you, "Why do you believe the Bible is true?" A lot of people answer that question by saying, "Because I have faith!" Is that a good answer, though? Does your belief about anything change whether or not it's true? As Frank Turek says, "If you don't believe in gravity, do you float away?" No, that's not how it works. Whether I believe in the Bible or not doesn't change a thing about whether or not it is true. So, we're not going to get anywhere with nonbelievers if we just say, "I have faith in the Bible and that's why I believe it's true." There's more to it than that. There's evidence.

I believe that science points to God, not away from Him. Science proves that the universe had a beginning. I believe it must have had a "Beginner." History definitely points to God. Even the biggest skeptic would have to admit that the popularity of Jesus worldwide for thousands of years is tough to explain if He didn't exist. Even mathematics, archaeology, and morality point to God. The fact that Christianity exploded *after* Jesus's death is evidence it really happened. The writers of Scripture included real people, real places, and embarrassing things about themselves, which is another kind of proof. The incredible design of the universe and the human body point to God; I don't believe these things could've just happened.

In the first century, Christians were being persecuted for their faith. One of the leaders who wasn't a follower of Jesus was a man named Gamaliel. He gave this warning to the people in Jerusalem in Acts 5:36–37:

> *Some time ago Theudas appeared, claiming to be somebody, and about four hundred men rallied to him. He was killed, all his followers were dispersed, and it all came to nothing. After him, Judas the Galilean appeared in the days of the census and led a band of people in revolt. He too was killed, and all his followers were scattered.*

Basically, Gamaliel was saying that every so often, a new "religion" or "movement" comes along, and people get all excited. But once the leader dies, the movement dies too. So that could have happened with the followers of Jesus too, right? Gamaliel then said this:

> *Therefore, in the present case I advise you: Leave these men alone! Let them go! For if their purpose or activity is of human origin, it will fail. But if it is from God, you will not be able to stop these men; you will only find yourselves fighting against God.*

—Acts 5:38–39

If the Christian movement is really of God, nobody will be able to stop it. Guess what? Here we are, a few thousand years later talking about the same God. He will not be stopped.

Am I saying there's 100 percent proof of God that you can show to a nonbeliever? No, that's not what I'm saying. But I am saying that there is evidence for our faith. And the more we study, the more we see how big God is, how incredible God is, and how much He continues to communicate to us through His creation, through His people, through our experiences, and through His Word. And yes, our faith is often about things we cannot see, but it's about being sure and certain of the evidence that we do have.

Too often, we let fear get in the way of true faith. Being afraid from time to time is normal. You could argue that if we're never fearful of anything, we're probably not doing enough with our faith to begin with. Was I afraid when I moved across the country by myself for a job? Absolutely. But I didn't let my fear outweigh my faith. We can't let our fear call the shots.

Being sure and certain of our faith also doesn't mean things will always go as planned. As much as I would love to have all the answers figured out in life, I never will. The sooner I realize that God is God, and I'm Tyler, the better off I will be.

Remember the faith of the men in the fiery furnace? Their response still astounds me to this day. When they were ordered to bow down to a king or be put to death, here's what they said:

If we are thrown into the blazing furnace, the God we serve is able to deliver us from it, and he will deliver us from Your Majesty's hand. But even if he does not, we want you to know, Your Majesty, that we will not serve your gods or worship the image of gold you have set up.

—Dan. 3:17–18

How incredible is this story? First of all, the boldness of these men to be able to stand up when everybody else is bowing down shows unbelievable faith in itself. But then, they say that their God is able to save them, "but *even if he does not*," they will still worship Him and not the king.

When they were admitting that God may or may not save them from the fire, that doesn't mean their faith was small. It means their faith was *massive*. Because they trusted in God's plan even if it wasn't what they wanted.

Too often, our faith gets shattered when tragedy strikes in our lives. That shouldn't be the case.

My brother-in-law has cancer. God is good.

This is not a contradiction.

There is violence, racism, war, hatred, sickness, and skepticism all around us. None of this changes the goodness of God. Some would argue that these things prove God isn't real. One little problem with that belief: the Bible predicted all these things. We aren't promised a happy life on earth. We aren't even promised tomorrow. But we are promised that God will be with us in the midst of our pain. And we're promised an eternal joy for all who believe.

I don't have all the answers, but I have enough faith to get in the wheelbarrow that Jesus is holding. There's plenty of evidence of His existence if we really look for it. My life is finite: I'm going to trust the infinite.

As Paul said in Galatians 5:6, "The only thing that counts is faith expressing itself through love." Did you catch that? He didn't say our accomplishments count. He didn't say the number of our Instagram followers counts. He didn't say the number in our bank account matters. He said the **only** thing that counts is faith, expressing itself through love. In other words: faith in action is all that really matters. If we sincerely want to search for God, faith in action is required.

Faith and love aren't supposed to be only about beliefs and feelings. They are both supposed to be action words. Spend 15 minutes in Hebrews 11 and look at the action involved with all the heroes of our faith. Look up other stories in the New Testament and take note what faith in action looks like.

I don't know about you, but I tend to treat things differently when I own them or worked for them. If your parents give you 20 bucks to spend at a football game, you might blow that money in a matter of minutes and not think twice about it. If you had to work a few hours on a farm to earn that money, you'd probably put a little more thought into how to spend it. If I purchase something with my own money, I'm going to take really good care of it. Our faith can be like that too. If you really own your faith and it's not your parents', friend's, or spouse's faith, you'll treat it differently. You'll be more likely to care for it and put it to use.

Living out our faith won't be easy, and it was never meant to be. We don't put action to our faith for God to love us. He already loves us. We put action to our faith to grow and to show it's real. We put action to our faith to reach others. We put action to our faith because it's the only thing that really matters in this life.

Our faith is not a blind faith. I can be sure and certain in Jesus. And He's asking us to get in the wheelbarrow.

Chapter Four

Just Say Yes

Several years ago, a traveling reality theater production called *The 99* came to my town. It was a walk-through theater that graphically reenacted the five leading causes of death in teenagers and young adults in the United States. I didn't know anything about this production, but it sounded intriguing, so I went to a meeting along with many other pastors from the surrounding communities.

At the meeting, they told us this production would attract between 10,000 and 20,000 people, and they would need at least 200 volunteers per night. This reality theater would take place inside a 20,000-square-foot tent, typically placed in a mall parking lot. The best part? Of the 10,000 to 20,000 people who would attend, 70 to 80 percent of them would be unchurched, and this production shares the gospel with every single one of them.

Each group of people would go through several rooms and experience scenarios that were either 5 1/2 minutes or 11 minutes long. They would see real-life events portrayed by actors. Toward the end of the production was a room that represented hell, followed by a Ministry Room, and a final room full of pastors and counselors available to talk to everyone about what they had just experienced.

It sounded like an amazing thing, so I signed up. I told them to put me down for whatever they needed me to do.

Be careful what you wish for! Next thing I knew, they told me, "Tyler, I'm not sure if you'd be okay with this or not, but we really need your help in the Ministry Room."

Now, I was in ministry at the time. But I was young and wasn't always the most outgoing or confident person with people outside my own group. Imagine being asked to share the gospel with thousands of unchurched people who didn't know they were about to hear it. "Would these people be mad? Would they feel manipulated? Am I qualified? What if I mess up? Can't you find someone else who's better than me?" These were the thoughts running through my head.

Reluctantly, I still said yes. And guess what? It ended up being one of the most rewarding experiences of my entire life.

After going through some training, I was nervous but ready to give it a shot. In the Ministry Room, I had 11 minutes with each group that came in. Every 11 minutes, there would be a new group of people. I showed them a short video clip and then shared the gospel to the best of my ability. Most of the people were very receptive. Many of them cried. Many of them experienced a life-changing evening.

I can't stop thinking about how I almost said no. In my head, I was saying, "I'm not qualified to do this," or "I'm sorry, I just can't." I sounded a lot like Moses before he actually stepped up.

When God was trying to get Moses to step up and speak for Him, "Moses pleaded with the LORD, 'O Lord, I'm not very good with words. I never have been, and I'm not now, even though you have spoken to me. I get tongue-tied, and my words get tangled'" (Exod. 4:10 NLT). He was basically telling God, "You've got the wrong guy. I'm not fit for this. I can't do it."

Check out God's response:

The LORD said to him, "Who gave human beings their mouths? Who makes them deaf or mute? Who gives them sight or makes them blind?

Is it not I, the LORD? Now go; I will help you speak and will teach you what to say."

—Exod. 4:11–12

Let's recap: Moses says, "I can't speak for You." God says, "I'm the One that made your mouth, so I know you can." Maybe we should stop telling God what we can't do.

Because I said yes, I had the opportunity to speak to thousands of people about Jesus. I was so impacted by this experience I wanted to do more. The next city that *The 99* was headed to was Louisville, Kentucky. I drove three hours and stayed overnight in Louisville the next weekend, just so I could work in the Ministry Room for another two nights in a different city.

This was a turning point in my faith. From that point on, I started saying yes to more things that were faith-related. Instead of making excuses and finding ways out, I started thinking: "Maybe God wants me to do this. Maybe He's the one asking." Do you remember going to "Just Say No" rallies as a kid? Consider this your "Just Say Yes" rally. When it comes to opportunities in life, especially anything even remotely faith-related, say yes and watch God work.

The next time someone asks you to do something for the church or for an unchurched person, say yes. See what happens. Step out of your comfort zone. Even if you feel unqualified. Even if you think you're too busy. Even if it doesn't sound appealing at first. Go on that trip. Go to that service project. Go to that meeting and see what it's all about. Don't be afraid to go out on a limb—that's where the fruit is.

I always said I would never speak at funerals because I would be uncomfortable and wouldn't know what to say. So, the first time I was asked to do one was for my high school principal, a legend in the community, who passed away unexpectedly. I couldn't possibly say no to the family when they asked, and I felt like God put me in that position for a reason. I also spoke at the funeral of a friend who died in a car accident the following year. It was extremely difficult, but I'm thankful God helped me through it. I was able to share the gospel with many people, and I really felt like God gave me the right words at the right time. I don't know if the gospel would have been shared if I had declined. Instead of saying no, I knew God wanted me to step up in those situations.

For some people, it's easy to say yes to big adventures in life. I like to try new things. I take on new challenges. I like to travel. I like to set new goals each year. Studies show that experiences outweigh stuff, and I live by that. I spent 700 bucks to watch the Cubs win the pennant in 2016—money well spent. I spent 500 bucks to see U2 in concert for the first time—worth every penny. I know that life is short, and I want to experience everything this crazy life has to offer. That attitude needs to translate to my faith more often. Christianity is meant to be lived out. It's meant to be an adventure filled with risk and uncertainty but also with joy. Remember how Jesus's ministry was all about Him staying inside and preaching sermons in synagogues? Me neither.

What about the disciples? Did they play it safe? Not a chance. When Jesus gave them a mission, they said yes. Jesus may not speak to you audibly, but He may be trying to get your attention in other ways. When someone needs help or asks you to be part of something, it could be Him.

There are multiple verses in Scripture that tell us to make the most of every opportunity. We need to change our thinking sometimes. Instead of viewing something as an "obligation," view it as an "opportunity." You could even have that mentality for a school or work assignment. You're obligated to do it, but could it still be an opportunity? Absolutely.

Sometimes, I'll have my youth coaches or student leaders lead lessons at church. I give them that same advice. This is not a task. This is not busywork. This is an opportunity for you. Make the most of it.

Don't get me wrong; saying no is also important at times. Instead of doing 10 things half-heartedly, it would be better to do a few things really well. But we can't just say no to everything. We often say no to things we're not comfortable with or good at. You may be surprised what happens if you give it a chance. You can't walk on water without getting out of the boat, right?

I'm not searching for Jesus one day a week. I'm searching for Him all seven days. If He wants me to do something on a Tuesday morning or Thursday night, I want to say yes.

Chapter Five

It's Alive!

I've had some incredible experiences in my life as a sportswriter and concert promoter.

When I moved to Florida, I was worried that nobody there would talk to me about the sports teams that I love. So, I started a podcast and separate Twitter feed dedicated to those teams. It was an outlet for me and felt like a way to stay connected to a piece of home. I was able to build a nice little following of fans, and that helped me land a dream job. Justin Bieber was discovered on YouTube. I was discovered on Twitter. Pretty similar, right? Weeks after I moved back to Indiana, I received a phone call from a man named Cliff who told me he had started a website covering Indiana sports and asked if I wanted to take over. I thought about it for about three seconds and gladly accepted.

I became a sportswriter for the Indiana Pacers, Indiana Hoosiers, and other Indianapolis sporting events. I had season credentials, access to locker rooms, and the opportunity to interview the game's biggest stars. Being in the same room as LeBron James, Kobe Bryant, and Victor Oladipo? Sign me up. I was also able to cover the 2015 NCAA Final Four. I got to be on the floor right next to Mike Krzyzewski after Duke won the title that year.

I had another dream job when I was in college. I had the opportunity to work for Rockstock, a company that put on Christian concerts. I got to hang out backstage and on tour buses with artists such as Switchfoot, TobyMac, Relient K, Jeremy Camp, Newsboys, and many more.

Even though I've met and worked with a lot of celebrities, it would be a lie to say I am close friends with any of them. Many of the Pacers players know my name. Several Christian artists know who I am. But it would be a lie to say I really know these people on a personal level.

A lot of people know *of* God, but they don't really *know* Him. They may even have some experiences with God, but they don't really have a personal relationship with Him. It would be ridiculous for me to say, "LeBron James knows me really well because I've been in the same room as him several times!" That's like a lot of people saying, "I know God really well because I've been in a church building several times." It doesn't work that way. Knowing some things about Jesus or spending one hour a week with Him doesn't mean we really know Him.

Jesus desires a personal relationship with His children. I want to live my life searching for seven. I don't want to seek Him one day a week. I want to seek Him in every experience, all seven days. I want to hunger and thirst for His Word like it's the very food and water I need to survive.

Here's one solution for this pursuit: treat the Word of God like it's actually alive. Hebrews 4:12 says, "For the word of God is alive and active. Sharper than any double-edged sword." Too often, we treat it like it's old and dead instead of alive and active.

Simply knowing God's Word doesn't do much for us unless we know it's alive. Information means nothing unless that information changes us. The Jewish leaders of Jesus's day had the first five books of the Bible memorized. Many of the religious teachers had the entire Old Testament memorized. Can you even imagine that?

Did you get a sticker for memorizing a few Bible verses in Sunday school? Imagine reciting the entire Old Testament by memory. But who did Jesus get upset with the most in His lifetime? That's right—the religious leaders. The very people who had so much of God's Word memorized. How is that even possible? I believe they *knew* the Word but didn't really *know* the Word. They treated it like a spiritual checklist instead of a living Word. Jesus would explain to them that He was the fulfillment of the very words they had memorized, but they didn't want to believe it. Look at the world today. How many protestors have Bible verses on their signs that are taken out of context? You can know what the Bible says without really knowing what it means. Even Satan quoted Scripture in Matthew 4.

I can quote movie lines and song lyrics like it's my job. My wife pretends to be annoyed by this, but I think she secretly loves it. In almost any conversation, something will remind me of a lyric or movie quote. I want to be that way with God's Word. I don't want to just know *of* the words. I want to live *by* the words. Transformation is greater than information. I've spent a lot of time watching those movies and listening to those songs to be able to quote them. I need to spend more time in God's Word and treat it like it's alive. There's a big difference between reading the Bible like a textbook and "meditating on it day and night" (Ps. 1:2 NLT). I've also realized that I pick up on new things every time I rewatch a show or movie. Why would reading God's Word be any different?

I had a professor in college named Doc Henderson. He was 85 years old and still teaching. One day in class, he said something that I'll never forget. He said, "Every time I open God's Word, I learn something new." Simple enough, right? I've never met anyone more knowledgeable about the Bible than Doc Henderson. This guy could write in Hebrew and Greek at the same time using both hands. He had been teaching the Bible for 60+ years. For him to say that he learns something new every time he opens the Bible is a big deal.

When was the last time God's Word came alive for you?

I never dreamed I would move away from home but felt like God was preparing my heart to do so. I once had a job opportunity in Baltimore, and everything seemed to be lining up perfectly for it. A church in Baltimore paid for my flight to come visit for a full weekend. I met the staff, interviewed for the job, and everybody seemed to indicate I was the guy they wanted. A few days later, I received an email saying, "We loved everything about you, but we're not sure if you want to be here, so we're going to look in another direction." Looking back, I have a good idea why I didn't get the job. They had asked, "What does Indianapolis have that Baltimore doesn't?" So naturally, I said, "the Colts." They laughed, but we all know they were still hurting on the inside.

After getting that call, I was crushed and confused. Wasn't God preparing me for this? Why did I have this waste of time? The very next Sunday, the pastor at my church preached a sermon on Abraham and Isaac. It was a story I had heard a thousand times, but that day, it meant something entirely different to me. Why? Because God's Word is alive and active.

The pastor said, "Abraham showed God he was willing to do whatever the Lord asked, but God had other things in mind." When he said that, the story hit me like a bolt of lightning. It was like God was telling me, "You showed me you were willing to move away from home for Me, but I have something else in mind." Only a few months later, I received an even better job offer in Jacksonville, Florida. And I will never forget the way God spoke to me through His Word that Sunday. He can take a story you've heard a thousand times and breathe new life into those words on any given day.

The Bible is the only thing in the world that actually gets bigger the more you study it. If you go to college to study a subject, that subject is going to get smaller for you the more you study and understand it. That's not the case with God's Word. Continue to study it, and God will get even bigger.

In his novel *Prince Caspian*, C. S. Lewis wrote this gem:

"Aslan," said Lucy, "you're bigger."
"That is because you are older, little one," answered he.
"Not because you are?"
"I am not. But every year you grow, you will find me bigger."[1]

What a beautiful picture of the God I serve. That's what happens when we treat God and His Word as they should be treated—like they are alive.

In *Mere Christianity*, C. S. Lewis also said:

That is why daily prayers and religious readings and churchgoing are necessary parts of the Christian life. We have to be continually reminded of what we believe. Neither this belief nor any other will automatically remain alive in the mind. It must be fed.[2]

Our faith must be fed. The Apostle Paul wrote letters to churches to remind them of the gospel they already accepted. Accepting the message of Jesus is the first step. After that? It's up to us to continually feed our faith so we can grow.

Mindset Is Everything

One of my favorite things about youth ministry is taking kids to camps and conferences. Those are the main environments where life change takes place. I believe the main reason they are so impactful is because of the mindset of the students who attend. When you're at a camp or conference, you know what to expect. You know you're going to be there for a week with very little interaction with the outside world. You know you're going to be hearing about Jesus and talking about Jesus. So, for the most part, your mind is prepared to hear from God.

Many times, kids come back from camp and say things like, "The speaker at camp was amazing! They said we should read our Bibles!" Wow, what a novel concept! And as a youth pastor, you're thinking, "Seriously? I've been telling you that for years." The speakers at camp may say the exact same things as the pastors at church, but because of the environment and the mindset of the student, they may actually hear the message in those places.

So here's the question: How do we get that mindset every day of the week? Even preparing to hear from God on Sunday isn't enough. How do I prepare my heart and my mind to hear from God on a daily basis? There has to be good soil before good seed can do its work. Spending time with God and His Living Word would be a great place to start.

Reading other Christian books is great too. But as Charles Spurgeon once said, "Visit many books, but live in the Bible."[3]

The Word Is Your Miracle

Sometimes, we just want God to give us a sign. We want to experience a miracle. We want God to "show up" for us. Many people who lived in the time of Jesus wanted miracles too, even though they already experienced several of them. In Matthew 12:38–39, Jesus said no:

> *Then some of the Pharisees and teachers of the law said to him, "Teacher, we want to see a sign from you." He answered, "A wicked and adulterous generation asks for a sign! But none will be given it except the sign of the prophet Jonah."*

Think about what Jesus was saying here. Jonah was an Old Testament story. Jonah lived hundreds of years before these people. None of them were alive to see what Jonah experienced, yet Jesus told them Jonah was the only "sign" they needed.

Translation: "You want a sign? Read your Bible."

The Bible doesn't have every specific answer for your life. It's not going to tell you who to marry, what job to take, or things of that nature. But it can be the miracle we need. It can and should be one of the best ways we hear from God. We often want flashes in the sky or burning bush experiences, but God may be wanting to speak to you right now through His Word.

Too many Christians depend on church services alone for spiritual growth. It's great to hear what trustworthy people have to say about God's Word, but that can't be the only time we spend in it. A. W. Tozer said, "If your Christianity depends upon a pastor's preaching, then you're a long way from being where you should be."[4] If you need the fancy lights, loud music, and charismatic speaker to hear from God, you'll never know Him on the personal level He desires. It's on us to spend time with Him and grow in our faith. Let's keep searching for God each day through His Word. After all, it's alive.

Chapter Six
Illusions

When I was a senior in high school, I took a radio/TV class at a different school during the second half of the day. My friend Ian was also in the class, so we would ride together. We basically went out to eat every single day on the way to this class, and we would make funny voices at the drive-thru because we thought we were hilarious. We got to know some of the workers at Subway pretty well. They seemed to like us. Some of the other places weren't as amused at our humor.

At the end of the school year, we had this strange idea of making an award for one of the restaurants. We both decided that Arby's gave us the best service over the course of the year, so we made this fake award and put it in a frame. It read:

The Tyler and Ian Award
Congratulations, Arby's, best fast-food establishment
in Montgomery County

I mean, it looked somewhat official, but it was called the Tyler and Ian Award, which doesn't exactly scream legit. We didn't think anything would come of this, but when we went inside, we told them about the award. We said it was a school project, and they actually called the manager over. They wanted to get a picture with us! That's not even the crazy part. The crazy part is that they put this award on their wall, right by the register where people order—in plain sight for all to see. And that award, kid you not, was on the wall for over **four years**! A fake award that two kids made up—on a wall at Arby's for over four years. I would go into Arby's and say, "Hey, I'm Tyler from the Tyler and Ian Award!"

Years later, I was on a church softball team that won back-to-back league championships. We wanted to celebrate this incredible accomplishment in style, so we came up with an idea. The town where the church was located had a parade at the end of every summer, and our church had a float in the parade. Instead of just waving and passing out candy, we decided to treat this parade like it was our championship parade through town. We put our jerseys on and had our two trophies with us on the back of our float. We made a video and made it look like the town was putting on this huge parade for our church softball team. It confused a lot of people, and it was hilarious. I had multiple people say, "Your town actually threw you a championship parade for winning church league softball?" Naturally, I responded by saying, "Well, it wasn't just one title; it was back-to-back baby!" Good times.

Both of these stories just serve as a reminder to me that it can be so difficult to know what is real and what is fake in this life. It's a reminder that there are so many half-truths in the world, so many lies that we believe. And we end up believing so many things just because they look real or feel right.

Christians believe that total truth is found in Jesus. Total truth is found in God's Word. But as we try to navigate through life and find our identity in Him, it can be difficult because this world is full of illusions. Look no further than social media or the news and things you see on TV. We want to believe everything we see is true, but we know that's not always the case.

One of the biggest illusions for us to be aware of is the illusion of control. Surrender is such a big part of the Christian life. Giving up control and allowing God to really be the Lord of our life is what we need. It's about understanding that I'm not in control in this life. As much as I want to be in control, I'm not. There are very few things we can actually control ourselves. So, the only thing we can do is surrender and give God the control.

I'm not going to sugarcoat it: surrendering control is one of the hardest things in life to do. When we can't control things, we get upset. Think of these examples:

- When the weather makes you cancel your plans
- When traffic causes you to be late
- When another person's mistake impacts you in some way
- When the teacher gives you a pop quiz and you're not ready for it
- When you're playing a sport and a referee or umpire makes a horrible call or your teammate doesn't do their job

This list could go on and on, but the point is this: We like to be in control. We don't like to surrender. The word *surrender* is such a negative-sounding word. But as a Christian, it's supposed to be a beautiful word! The fact that I can't control very much in life and that I'm able to give it all to a God who can is supposed to be a beautiful thing!

It's like a child submitting to their parents. Do my kids ever think it's unfair that my wife and I have authority over them? Maybe sometimes when they don't want to go to bed or don't want to eat a certain thing. But they need us. They need to submit to our authority just to live. It should be the same way with us and God. We won't always like what we go through, and at times, we want to control situations, but He knows what's best. And surrendering to Him is actually a beautiful thing.

I want you to think about something: you live on a spinning blue planet that's floating in the middle of outer space. And I know you learn about that in school, but have you ever thought about that? You think you actually have any control in your life? You live on a big blue ball in the middle of nowhere in a massive solar system.

And if you compare the Earth to other stars, other planets, and other galaxies, we're like a little speck. We're just a little bitty dot compared to everything else. And you think you have control of anything in life?

You are absolutely relying on so many factors other than yourself to even be alive and to stay alive. And then when you pass away, what then? How much of that can you control? How much of your life and how much of your eternity is controlled by you?

Let's make a comprehensive list of things we can actually control in life:

- Your choices
- Your response to things that happen
- Your attitude
- How you treat other people

And that's about it. You can't always control what happens to you, but you can control how you respond to it. If we want to compare the things that we can control with the things we can't, there's really no comparison.

You didn't control when you were born or who your parents are or where you grew up. You won't control when you die. You can't control circumstances in life. You can't control the actions or choices of others. You can't control the weather, the economy, terrorism, or violence. The best thing you can do is to surrender everything to the God who can control all those things.

We serve a God who calmed the storms with His mouth! People were astonished, and they said, "Even the winds and waves obey him" (Matt. 8:27). And He doesn't just hold your life in His hands. He holds your eternal life in His hands. So, we have to stop trying to control everything.

Any time in my life when I've tried to control a situation, it typically hasn't worked out. Maybe God was reminding me: "Hey, I'm in control here, and you've got to give it to me. Don't try to fix

everything yourself; don't try to control this situation. Give it to me."
And I finally started listening.

Look at what it says in James 4:13–16 (ESV):

Come now, you who say, "Today or tomorrow we will go into such and such a town and spend a year there and trade and make a profit"—yet you do not know what tomorrow will bring. What is your life? For you are a mist that appears for a little time and then vanishes. Instead you ought to say, "If the Lord wills, we will live and do this or that." As it is, you boast in your arrogance. All such boasting is evil.

So, James says that we shouldn't even boast in our future plans. For we don't know what tomorrow holds. We should plan for the future; it's okay to plan for college, to save money, and to make plans for the upcoming weekend. But in James, we are taught to never boast in our plans. Our lives are like a mist. We're here for a little while and then we're gone. Some people hear that, and it makes them want to control their own circumstances even more. Instead, this should cause us to surrender.

We can get bad news in a split second. You can lose your life in a flash. How many people die in car accidents out of nowhere? Somebody else makes a mistake in their car, and your life could be over. Or somebody has a heart attack and dies within seconds. Or you get the news that you have cancer and you have just weeks to live. There's just no preparing for any of this. I don't say any of this to scare us or to make us feel upset. But we need to be aware of how fragile this life is. We're really not in control. And because this life is so fragile, that's why I don't want to live for this life, I want to live for eternity. As it says in Psalm 39:4, "Lord, remind me how brief my time on earth will be" (NLT). It is an illusion to believe we're in control in this life, so let's give it all to the God who is.

Another illusion in this life is that you are defined by your accomplishments or your failures. So many people either define themselves by something they've accomplished, or they define themselves by the biggest mistake they've ever made. It's an illusion to believe either one. The powers of darkness love it when we boast in something we did well, and they love it even more when we sulk in a past mistake.

Ecclesiastes is my favorite Old Testament book. It was written by King Solomon. And one thing we know about Solomon is that this dude was rich. In today's money, he made about $800 million per year and had a net worth of over $3 trillion. He was by far the richest and wisest man to ever live at that time. And yet look at what he writes in Ecclesiastes 2:7–11:

> *I also owned more herds and flocks than anyone in Jerusalem before me. I amassed silver and gold for myself, and the treasure of kings and provinces . . . I became greater by far than anyone in Jerusalem before me . . .*
>
> *I denied myself nothing my eyes desired;*
> *I refused my heart no pleasure.*
> *My heart took delight in all my labor,*
> *and this was the reward for all my toil.*
> *Yet when I surveyed all that my hands had done*
> *and what I had worked to achieve,*
> *everything was meaningless, a chasing after the wind;*
> *nothing was gained under the sun.*

King Solomon had everything. He was denied nothing. And yet he says that his accomplishments apart from God meant nothing. They were all meaningless. Your accomplishments don't define you. I'm not saying your accomplishments mean nothing; I'm saying your accomplishments apart from God mean nothing. I hope my accomplishments point people to my Creator. If they just point to myself, they'll eventually be long gone just like me.

Where do you see yourself five years from now? Don't you love/hate that question? Okay, how about this one: Where do you see yourself

100 years from now? Will people even know you existed? In 100 to 120 years from now, 100 percent of the people currently alive will be gone. What accomplishments are you really striving for anyway? And ask yourself this: Would you rather be remembered in 100 years because of a statue of yourself somewhere, or would you rather be in heaven and have someone come up to you and say, "Thank you for helping me find Jesus"? The latter is the kind of accomplishment we want to strive for the most. Do you want to be known by people when you're gone, or do you want to make Jesus known to the people in this life while you're alive?

Your failures don't define you either. This is the beauty of the gospel message! We don't deserve it. My salvation has nothing to do with me, and it has everything to do with the grace of God. And any time I've screwed up or fallen short, I can be forgiven. I'm no longer defined by my past or my sin or any mistakes I've made. If you follow Christ and are saved, God isn't going to look at your sin; He's going to see the cross.

Paul had Christians murdered. Peter disowned Jesus three times. The disciples screwed up over and over again. They were forgiven, and they followed Jesus, and they didn't dwell in their mistakes. The "religious" people wanted the "sinners" to be defined by their mistakes, and they wanted themselves to be defined by their accomplishments. Jesus had something else in mind. Let's be defined by Christ and not either one of those.

What about Jesus Himself? A lot of people think Jesus is the illusion. Maybe Christianity is the fake news. Maybe Christianity is the made-up story or the fabricated story. Did the miracles really happen or were they illusion?

There's an ancient historical Jewish text called the *Talmud* that says Jesus "practiced magic." So even though they weren't followers of Jesus, they wrote down in a historical document that a man named Jesus "practiced magic." By doing that, they admitted He was doing things they had never seen and things for which they had no explanation.

His miracles set Him apart from other prophets or teachers, or messengers of other religions. He performed miracles in part to prove He was who He said He was, but ultimately to lead people to Him.

Do miracles still happen today? Absolutely. Do they happen all the time? No. If they happened all the time, they wouldn't really make much of a difference. Some people believe the Bible is full of miracle after miracle, and that's simply not the case. There were some periods of hundreds of years in between miracles. So, if you ever ask God for a miracle and don't see one, maybe God's timing is different from yours. Maybe there's a bigger plan in place. Maybe we're praying with wrong motives. Or maybe it's just not in His will at that particular time, and we have to be okay with that.

The bottom line is this: We have a ton of historical evidence that Jesus was a real person, and that He performed real miracles, signs, and wonders. And in a world full of illusions such as we live in right now, people are going to try to tell you that Jesus is the made-up story, that **He** is the illusion. But Scripture actually predicted that would happen:

> *"Remember what I told you: 'A servant is not greater than his master.' If they persecuted me, they will persecute you also. If they obeyed my teaching, they will obey yours also"* (John 15:20).

> *"Blessed are you when people insult you, persecute you and falsely say all kinds of evil against you because of me"* (Matt. 5:11).

> *I urge you, brothers and sisters, to watch out for those who cause divisions and put obstacles in your way that are contrary to the teaching you have learned. Keep away from them* (Rom. 16:17).

It's no secret that a lot of people in America are leaving the church and faith behind, especially young adults in the millennial and Gen Z age ranges. One of the top reasons they give for leaving the church is that they believe people are fake. They don't see enough transparency. If we want to make a difference for Christ, we need to be real. We need to be transparent. We need to stop pretending. Let's stop pretending like we have it all figured out. Stop pretending that my sin is better than your sin. Stop pretending that being a Christian is about your behavior and your good deeds. Instead, we need to be real with people and share about our struggles, doubts, questions, and fears. This world doesn't need any more pretenders or they're just going to think our faith is the illusion. What they need are real, genuine, honest people who aren't afraid to admit their shortcomings—people who are transparent about their brokenness and their need for a Savior. That's a challenge for all of us.

One final illusion to discuss, and it's a big one. It's the illusion Satan wants you to believe. It's the one that says, "You're not good enough. You're not worth anything."

Jesus went to a cross to show you how valuable you really are. Our identity is in Christ alone. I have several jobs, projects, and different things I'm involved in. Not one of them defines who I am. And there will always be people better than me at each thing. But my identity isn't in what I do. Every time we think we aren't good enough in this life, go back and reflect on those red letters in Scripture especially. Who does Jesus say I am? That's what matters.

My purpose in writing is simply this: that you who believe in God's Son will know beyond the shadow of a doubt that you have eternal life, the reality and not the illusion. And how bold and free we then become in his presence, freely asking according to his will, sure that he's listening. And if we're confident that he's listening, we know that what we've asked for is as good as ours.

—1 John 5:13–15 MSG

Amen.

Chapter Seven

Platforms and Talents

I was a show choir kid growing up. Before you make fun of me, you have to understand something: show choir was cool at my school. No really, it was! Four of the five starters on the basketball team were in show choir. Lots of football players and cheerleaders were as well. Am I saying this to make myself feel better? Maybe. But that's beside the point.

It was a fun experience, especially going to competitions. I had a solo my senior year, which was one of my many attempts to get girls to like me.

At the end of every school year, we had our big Spring Show. We would perform our competition show that night, but we would also have lots of new material to perform. There was also an opportunity for lots of students to sing additional solos, and you could pick whatever song you wanted.

MercyMe's song "I Can Only Imagine" was really popular at that time, and I had recently performed that song at my church. So, my family encouraged me to choose that song for my final Spring Show. This would have been a great opportunity to share a song about Jesus with my fellow classmates and the crowd. I had a platform, and I could have used it to share about my faith.

But instead, I chose to sing a song to a girl who would be in attendance. She wasn't even someone I had been dating for a long time or someone I had a realistic chance of marrying one day. I was okay singing a song about Jesus at church. I wasn't brave enough to sing that song at my school. God laid an opportunity to give Him glory on a tee for me, and I whiffed.

Can you give Him glory singing a song that isn't Christian? Of course. We can glorify Him in many ways, every day of our lives. But looking back, I regret not singing "Imagine" when I should have.

The truth is, God gives all of us different platforms and talents. He then gives us the choice of how we're going to use them. What platforms has He given you? What platforms do you have right now?

When some people think of platforms, they may think of celebrities or people with thousands of followers on social media. When I think of platforms, I think of any opportunity you have to reach another person.

If you have coworkers of any kind, you have a platform.

If you are on a team of any kind, you have a platform.

If you have classmates, you have a platform.

If you have friends, neighbors, and family members, those are all platforms.

Back to show choir because I know you love it.

I once had a student ask me how he could reach his friends. I told him to use the platforms God has given him to reach those groups of people. This student was in show choir, so I told him to love his show choir classmates like Jesus would. God gave him the ability to sing and dance, which gave him about 30 classmates that he otherwise wouldn't have spent much time with. Does this mean he should sing and dance while he shares the gospel? Does he have to sing "Jesus Loves Me" to use that platform? Of course not. But using that platform means sharing Jesus with that group of people, since God had given him that opportunity.

In Matthew 25:14–29, Jesus taught the parable of the talents. There was a master who trusted three of his servants, and he gave each of them some talents (money) to put to use. He gave one servant five talents, another servant two talents, and another servant one talent. The first two put their talents to use, and they were rewarded. The last servant didn't do anything with his talent, and he was thrown out by the master. I believe Jesus was teaching that we all have different talents, and we're all called to put them to use. Every gift or talent God has given you is for a reason. Did he give you a good singing voice? Use it to glorify Him. Did He give you athletic ability? Mechanical skills? Book smarts? The gift of teaching? Artistic ability? Whatever He gave you, use that platform for Him in some way.

According to the parable of the talents, when we put our talents to use, we'll all get the same reward. That means a mega-church pastor and a small-town pastor will get the same reward, as long as they were both faithful and put their talents to use. If God is calling you to share the gospel with a coworker and you are faithful with that, you can get the same reward reaching one person as someone else who is called to reach thousands. The key is being faithful and putting what God has given us to work. That doesn't always seem right to us, but it's what Jesus taught. His grace isn't always fair. Thank God for that.

So God wants to use me in my strengths. He also wants to use me in my weaknesses. Sometimes, His power can be better displayed when my "ability" doesn't get in the way. I'm still called to be faithful and bring everything I've got, just like the boy who had some fish and some bread. He simply brought what he had, and Jesus multiplied it. Believe it or not, our weaknesses are platforms too.

In 2 Corinthians 12:9, Paul says, "But he [Jesus] said to me, 'My grace is sufficient for you, for my power is made perfect in weakness.' Therefore I will boast all the more gladly about my weaknesses, so that Christ's power may rest on me."

Society tells you to hide your weaknesses and your shortcomings. We're taught to show people the good and leave out the bad. Don't bother people with your problems, right? Scripture says otherwise.

In my weakness, His power shines through. I'm even told to boast about my weakness to show what God has done in my life. Whatever you struggle with or whatever mistakes you've made, don't be afraid to name them. Don't be afraid to use them. Like the woman at the well, go tell the whole town about your past because your weaknesses no longer define you, thanks to Jesus. If you've been healed, show off your scars and give God the glory.

As Lecrae says, "The only way to begin nursing your wounds is by naming them. If you ignore your wounds, they won't go away. What happens to you doesn't define you, but it can kill you if you ignore it."[1]

Your biggest platform in life might be from a mistake you made or a struggle you've had to deal with. I'm searching for seven, even when I fall down seven times. "Though the righteous fall seven times, they rise again" (Prov. 24:16).

What are your talents? What are your weaknesses? They're both opportunities. When you're good at something, let the world know it was a gift from God. When you screw something up, let the world know how He forgave you and showed up in your weakness.

When Jesus called us salt and light, we have to remember how important salt and light were to the people of that time. We also have to remember that salt and light are never meant to be the focus. They are meant to accentuate something else that's greater. Can you imagine if you walked in on somebody eating a bowl of salt? Or can you imagine going to an art exhibit and instead of looking at the painting, your friend is just staring at the light instead? Jesus said, "Let your light shine before others, that they may see your good deeds and glorify your Father in heaven" (Matt. 5:16).

He gets the glory, not us. Be salt and light and keep the focus on Him. Your platforms will change in your life. Don't miss the ones you have right now.

Chapter Eight
Choose the Right Battles

"Blessed are the peacemakers" (Matt. 5:9). Jesus said those words in the most famous sermon in history. I'm sure it was difficult to follow those words in the first century, and I know it's difficult in the twenty-first century. There's a lot of division in the world today, and that includes among churches and Christians—people who are supposed to be on the same team.

The writer of Hebrews said, "Make every effort to live in peace with everyone and to be holy; without holiness, no one will see the Lord" (Heb. 12:14).

Ask yourself these questions: Have I been making every effort to live in peace with everyone? Am I a peacemaker? Am I part of the problem or the solution? What about the people who have wronged me? What about the people who voted differently than me? What about the people who believe something that I just can't support?

These verses don't exclude anyone. To take it a step further, the Apostle Paul said we have the "ministry of reconciliation" (2 Cor. 5:18). To reconcile means to bring two things together. It means to take two things that are broken and help restore them. We have an actual ministry in this life, a ministry of reconciliation.

One of the reasons we are so bad at following these verses is because we don't always choose the right battles to fight. Take something like the age of the Earth debate. It's a fun topic to discuss, and it can be interesting. But it's not a salvation issue. It's not worth a big argument. People have actually left churches over this? There's also a lot of debate over Revelation and when/how the world will end.

Here's the truth:

Genesis is more about *who* made the earth instead of when it was made.

Revelation is more about *who* wins instead of the time of victory.

Let's spend more time figuring out how to share Jesus with the world instead of bickering over an issue that has nothing to do with our salvation.

How about the topic of politics? Is it even possible to "live in peace with everyone" when it comes to something as divisive as politics? The answer needs to be yes. When I look at social media, it seems like a lot of Christians care more about proving a point than they care about sharing Jesus. Instead of approaching those conversations with grace and actually trying to hear the other side out, people just want to win an argument.

As Bob Goff says, "It will be our love, not our opinions, which will be our greatest contribution to the world."[1] He also said, "Sadly, whenever I make my opinions more important than the difficult people God made, I turn the wine back into water."[2]

I believe Jesus cares deeply about political topics. But you know what? He cares about people more. And believe it or not, there is a way to stand up for what you believe but in a loving way.

Andy Stanley says, "Most bad church experiences are the result of somebody prioritizing a VIEW over a YOU, something Jesus never did and instructed us not to do either."[3] How many problems in the world and in the church would be solved if we'd simply think about the person first, and our opinion second?

If you ask my opinion, Goff and Stanley belong on the Mount Rushmore of Christian authors. Timothy Keller belongs on it too. In an article for the *New York Times*, Keller said it would be a huge mistake to call either political party the "Christian" party. He said if you look at the book of Acts, some of the things the early church fought for would seem to align more with Republicans, and some of the things they fought for would align more with Democrats.[4]

I have friends on both sides of every debate, both Christian, and non-Christian. I want to do my absolute best to listen to both sides, share my opinion only when it's necessary, and to do it with patience and respect. On the other side of an argument could be a hurting soul that just wants to be heard. Maybe that person is dead wrong. Maybe they are misinformed. Maybe they have something to offer that I should listen to. Regardless, the goal should be to approach each conversation in a Christlike way. Do I want to win an argument and look good? Or do I want to share Christ?

I love my country, and I'm proud to be an American. I'm so thankful for the men and women who have fought for our freedom. At the same time, it's really confusing when I see some Christians caring more about America than their faith. Are you prouder to be an American or a child of God? We need to get our priorities straight.

I've seen people leave their church because women were allowed to pass the communion plates. Is that the hill you really want to die on? I've seen Christians treat the LGBTQ community like they are the scum of the earth. You don't have to agree with someone to love them. Does a person have a better chance of changing if you love them and show them Christ or if you try to guilt them into a rules-based faith?

When I see Christians getting "outraged" on social media over extremely minor issues, it sickens me. Who cares if Starbucks won't say Merry Christmas? Who cares if a non-Christian business doesn't do Christian things? Oh, you're going to boycott a movie because of what one of the actors said? Who cares?

If we want to come across as petty, arrogant, ignorant, or hateful, we're doing a great job.

If we want to come across as followers of Christ, we should really think about choosing the right battles.

Should we hold one another accountable when we sin? Absolutely. There's a time and place for healthy confrontation. But when we try to guilt someone into following Jesus, that conversation will go nowhere. In 2 Timothy 2:22, Paul says, "Flee the evil desires of youth and pursue righteousness, faith, love and peace, along with those who call on the Lord out of a pure heart." Yes, we are called to flee sin and make every effort to do so. But we're also called to pursue our faith and righteousness. Let's help each other with our sin, but let's do it by pursuing Christ instead of legalism.

Everything we say or do can have an impact on others. This is true for the present and the future. When my church was going through a rough time, I didn't agree with a lot of the decisions that were being made. A lot of people upset me. But I got up onstage and told the congregation we needed to be unified. I told them:

> Whether you agree or disagree with what is happening, you have a role to play in this. How you respond to all of this won't just impact this church today. It could have a big impact on people that walk through that door 10 years from now.

Even in disagreements, how we "battle" is just as important as what we're battling. Scripture says we should be "quick to listen and slow to speak" (James 1:19). Many people have that reversed. Speaking your mind is sometimes a good thing, and sometimes, it's a bad thing. The same can be said for staying quiet. So few can find the balance.

There are a lot of things worth fighting for in this life. Stand up for what you believe and follow your convictions. But when we fight for something, let's do it with the heart of Christ. Let's get "outraged" over sex trafficking, world hunger, and the water crisis instead of trivial things on social media. Let's be peacemakers. Let's focus more on salvation issues than debate over the things that don't really matter.

The greatest battle ever was won at Calvary in AD 33. Jesus didn't die so we could fight over minor issues. We have a choice: Win arguments, or win people? Choose wisely.

Chapter Nine

Seven Times Seventy Times

A few years back, I created a DVD curriculum series called *Alektor*, which you can purchase online. It's a three-week series that helps teens learn how to keep their faith strong after they graduate. I was able to interview Jeremy Camp, former Newsboy Phil Joel, the chaplain of the Indianapolis Colts, and numerous pastors and students from all over the country. My favorite part of the entire process was interviewing Eric Smallridge.

At the time, Eric was serving an 11-year prison sentence. He made the huge mistake of driving while drunk when he was in college, and as a result, two 20-year-old women were killed. He was originally given a 22-year sentence. A few years into serving his time, however, the mother of one of the deceased women came forward and asked the judge to reduce his sentence. The mother's name is Renee Napier. She told CBS News, "I could hate him forever and the world would tell me that I have a right to do that. In my opinion, forgiveness is the only way to heal."[1]

Eric became a Christian while in prison. He and Renee go around to schools all over the country teaching about the importance of making good choices and the power of forgiveness. Matthew West's song "Forgiveness" is about this very story. It's an unbelievable reminder how we can forgive others in the most unthinkable circumstances because of the forgiveness Christ offers us.

When I interviewed Eric, I told him, "Even though you're in shackles and chains right now, you're more free than most people I know." Being forgiven by Christ is the ultimate freedom.

Here's an amazing truth: The second you come to Christ is the second you are forgiven.

The woman at the well had had five husbands and was living with another man. She had a conversation with Jesus, and she walked away forgiven.

Zacchaeus was a chief tax collector, despised by the people for taking too much of their money. He met Jesus, and he walked away forgiven.

How about the criminal who was on the cross next to Jesus? He asked for mercy, and Jesus told him he would join Him in paradise. If you think you've done too much to be forgiven, the Bible tells another story.

Romans 5:8 says, "While we were still sinners, Christ died for us." It doesn't say, "Get your life right and then come to Jesus." He died for you and for me, knowing we were sinners, knowing we'd continue to be sinners, and knowing we were still worth it.

There's a parable that Jesus taught in Matthew 18:23–35 that is powerful:

"Therefore, the kingdom of heaven is like a king who wanted to settle accounts with his servants. As he began the settlement, a man who owed him ten thousand bags of gold was brought to him. Since he was not able to pay, the master ordered that he and his wife and his children and all that he had be sold to repay the debt.

"At this the servant fell on his knees before him. 'Be patient with me,' he begged, 'and I will pay back everything.' The servant's master took pity on him, canceled the debt and let him go. But when that servant went out, he found one of his fellow servants who owed him a hundred silver coins. He grabbed him and began to choke him. 'Pay back what you owe

me!' he demanded. His fellow servant fell to his knees and begged him, 'Be patient with me, and I will pay it back.' But he refused. Instead, he went off and had the man thrown into prison until he could pay the debt.

"When the other servants saw what had happened, they were outraged and went and told their master everything that had happened. Then the master called the servant in. 'You wicked servant,' he said, 'I canceled all that debt of yours because you begged me to. Shouldn't you have had mercy on your fellow servant just as I had on you?' In anger his master handed him over to the jailers to be tortured, until he should pay back all he owed.

"This is how my heavenly Father will treat each of you unless you forgive your brother or sister from your heart."

The servant was forgiven of a debt he could never repay. He should have no problem forgiving others then too, right? You would think. Instead, the first chance he gets to display that forgiveness, he refuses. In today's money, he was forgiven a debt of billions of dollars, and he then wouldn't forgive the person who owed him $1,000.

We can point the finger at this person all we want. But his story is often our story, isn't it? We've been forgiven a debt we could never repay, but we still hold grudges with that person who made fun of us in high school or said something mean about us.

I remember having car problems in college. Every time I would take the car to the shop, they would say they found a new problem. I would pay them to fix it, and I'd be on my way. But the problem kept returning. My car would die in the middle of a busy intersection, and I would have to get it towed. Obviously, they weren't fixing the problem, and I kept paying them to not fix my car. I'm not one of those people who typically talks to my vehicle, but I did this time. When it died for the fifth time, I said to my car, "Are you kidding me? I thought you were fixed!"

I wonder how many times God thinks the same thing about me when I continue to let Him down. "Are you kidding me, Tyler? I forgave you for that. I thought you were fixed." I keep letting Him down, but yet He keeps on forgiving me. And as tough as it was for me to forgive the men who weren't fixing my car, I had to remind myself of the bigger story in my life.

Oddly enough, I got T-boned by a lady who ran a red light shortly after that. It was a scary moment. Thankfully, nobody was hurt. I don't recommend it, but hey, that was one way to take care of my continuous car problem!

In one of his conversations with Jesus, Peter asked Him, "Lord, how many times shall I forgive my brother or sister who sins against me? Up to seven times?" Jesus answered, "I tell you, not seven times, but seventy-seven times" (Matt. 18:21–22).

And no, He didn't mean 490 times. That number signified His eternal forgiveness.

If I'm going to search for seven in my life, I should always be reminded of the seven times seventy times principle. Forgiveness should be front and center on my to-do list. There's no other way around it. I have no right to ask God to forgive me for every sin I've ever committed if I can't forgive someone else who wronged me a handful of times.

Have you ever prayed the Lord's prayer? Think about what you're saying if you do. When it gets to the part where you say, "Forgive us our debts, as we forgive our debtors," you are actually telling God that you're okay being forgiven in the same manner in which you forgive other people. That can be a terrifying thought. Maybe it will wake us up.

How important is forgiveness in a marriage? How important is forgiveness as a parent? How important is forgiveness in a church? We will never experience God's completeness without it. We will never live the life He intended without it. And if we want to share

Christ with the world, displaying His forgiveness is one of those non-negotiables.

How serious is this to God? Look at what Jesus said in Matthew:

If you enter your place of worship and, about to make an offering, you suddenly remember a grudge a friend has against you, abandon your offering, leave immediately, go to this friend and make things right. Then and only then, come back and work things out with God.

—Matt. 5:23–24 MSG

How serious is this to God? He'd rather you leave your time of worship and make things right with someone instead of staying to worship while still holding a grudge against them. That's how serious this is to God.

In our pursuit of forgiving others, maybe we need to spend a little more time reflecting on how much we've been forgiven. One day, I'm going to stand before my Maker. In that moment, I could give Him a list of all my "spiritual accomplishments." I could say, "God, look at everything I did for you! I wrote a book! I played Jesus in an Easter drama! I did youth ministry for X number of years! I preached about you to thousands of people! I have curriculum for other pastors online! This is all good enough to get me in the door, right?"

Wrong.

I will not be going to heaven one day because of my "spiritual résumé." None of that is enough. None of that compares to the perfection of God.

I'm saved and I'm going to heaven for all eternity because of one reason, and one reason only: the forgiveness of my Savior. I want my life to be an offering and reflection of that unbelievable forgiveness.

Forgive us our debts, as we forgive our debtors—seven times seventy times.

Amen.

Chapter Ten
Contentment

Imagine a friend inviting you on a camping trip one weekend. Your friend tells you, "All you need to bring is a sleeping bag. Everything else is covered." So, you assume that your friend is telling the truth, and the only thing you pack is your sleeping bag. When you get to the campsite, you realize you definitely needed more than your sleeping bag. To make things worse, your friend has everything: a blow-up mattress, a flashlight, bug spray, a fluffy pillow, a personal fan, and some snacks. And then your friend tells you they aren't sharing any of it. "You told me all I needed was a sleeping bag, but clearly that's not true! It looks like you actually need all this other stuff to go camping here."

Unfortunately, this story is pretty similar to how a lot of Christians live their lives. They tell their friends, "All you need is Jesus! You don't need anything else!" But when their friends look at their lives, that's not what they see. They may say, "How can you tell me that all you need is Jesus when your life shows that you actually need all this other stuff? If all you need is Jesus, why does your life indicate you need money to be happy, or success, or popularity, or the approval of other people? It sure doesn't seem like 'all you really need is Jesus' when your life says otherwise."

As a Christian, our very identity, our very DNA, lies in Jesus Christ. He really is all we need. I want to encourage you to live a life that shows He really is all we need. Even when I'm going through the hardest of times, I'm still content because I am a forgiven soul who is saved by the blood of Jesus. Even if I'm doing really well and have lots of money, I want my life to show Jesus is enough.

Paul knew how to be content in every situation. Philippians 4:13 is one of the most quoted verses in the entire Bible. It can be taken out of context at times, but it's a beautiful verse when used correctly: "I can do all things through Christ who gives me strength." What Paul says before that verse is really important:

> *I am not saying this because I am in need, for I have learned to be content whatever the circumstances. I know what it is to be in need, and I know what it is to have plenty. I have learned the secret of being content in any and every situation, whether well fed or hungry, whether living in plenty or in want.*
>
> —Phil. 4:11–12

And then he says, "I can do all things through Christ who gives me strength." So, when you think of that verse, think about what comes before it. Paul was rich and powerful at times in his life, and at other times he was poor, beaten, persecuted, and thrown into prison. So, in this passage, Paul is saying, "I know what it's like to have a lot . . . and believe me, I know what it's like to have nothing . . . but I've learned to be content in every situation. Why? Because I can do all things through Him who gives me strength."

I believe that even in someone's earthly death, we are called to be content. This may sound like a really strange thing to say, but I believe it to be true. Now, we're taught that it's healthy to mourn that kind of loss, and I'm not saying it's supposed to make us happy. What I'm saying is this: we are not a product of time; we are a product of eternity. If we are a product of eternity and not time on earth, then maybe God's healing came in our loved one's earthly death. Think about this: our citizenship as believers is in heaven. Maybe we prayed for a loved one to be healed, and God's healing was through their death so they could live with Him, with no more pain, and no more problems.

In truth, Jesus cares far more about our spiritual needs than our physical needs. Does He care about our physical needs? Of course, He does. He cares deeply about every single part of us. But He cares the most about our spiritual needs. A story from Scripture that I think about a lot is the story of Jesus feeding the 5,000. When Jesus fed the 5,000, many of those people came to search for Jesus in the days and weeks afterward. But many of them weren't searching for Him because they wanted to make Him Lord of their lives. They were trying to find Him because they simply wanted more food. They were missing the point. Jesus didn't feed them just so their physical needs would be met. When we eat, we'll be filled, but we'll just be hungry again later that day. Jesus fed them to show them their spiritual needs could be met through Him. So, think about that. If Jesus cares more about our spiritual needs than our physical needs, that means sometimes our physical needs will not be met, and maybe there's a larger purpose being played out.

God doesn't promise that we won't go through pain. He just promises to be with us in the midst of it. There was a man who was born blind back in Jesus's day, and, in John 9:2, the disciples asked Jesus, "Who sinned, this man or his parents, that he was born blind?" A lot of people in that day assumed that good things happened to good people, and bad things happened to bad people. There are people today who still believe that, but it was even more of the case back then. So, the disciples assumed that someone must have had a pretty bad sin to make this man blind from birth. But look at Jesus's response in John 9 verse 3: "Neither this man nor his parents sinned . . . but this happened so that the works of God might be displayed in him." Here's another example of how we are a product of eternity, and not time.

This man was born blind for a purpose. Not because he was bad, but so that God's power may be displayed in his life. I want to remember this story the next time something bad happens in my life. Instead of blaming ourselves or blaming God for something, let's remember this story and realize that there could be a reason behind what is happening. Maybe this is happening so that God's power can be displayed. I can be content with what is happening right now because God will use this to reveal His power to other people if we allow Him to do so.

Being content in all things is a matter of the heart. I didn't get married until the age of 30, and I even went to a Bible college! Everybody gets married at Bible college, right? Not this guy. And at times, I was okay with that. Other times, it was hard to be content. I had a few relationships that felt like they would last. I even went to my girlfriend's house and asked her parents for their blessing to marry her when I was 20 years old. Things came crashing down shortly after that in our relationship, and I'm glad they did. But at the time, I was crushed. Several relationships, hard breakups, and years later, I finally found the woman I would marry. Trusting in God's timing isn't always easy, but it's a whole lot better than trusting in our own.

For you, it may be an entirely different example. Maybe it's hard to be content at work. Maybe it's hard to be content with finances. Maybe it's hard to be content with your current circumstances in some way. Let's remember the words of Paul, and let's learn the secret of being content in all things, which is only found in Jesus Christ. We can do all things through Him who gives us strength.

Psalm 23:1 (ESV) says, "The LORD is my shepherd; I shall not want." The NIV translation says, "The LORD is my shepherd, I lack nothing." A question that you may have to ask yourself today is: If the Lord is your Shepherd, why are you still living in want? If the Lord is our Shepherd, why would we ever live like we are lacking anything? I don't know what your situation is, but I know most of us don't think enough about how blessed we are. No matter how much money I have or don't have, I'm filthy rich, because my Father owns everything. And He not only owns everything, but He loves me. And He saw enough in me to die on a cross. Why would we still live our lives as if that's not enough? Why would we still be in want?

One of my favorite worship songs growing up was a song called, "Better Is One Day." It's a song that comes from Psalm 84:10, which says: "Better is one day in your courts, than a thousand elsewhere." We will have good days, and we will have bad days on this earth. But let's live by that verse and know what awaits us. Think about some of the best days of your life—the day of your first kiss; the day you got your driver's license; the day the Cubs won the World Series; the day you graduated; the day you got married; the day you had a child; the day you got a big promotion. Now, lump all your best days together. Put a thousand of them together even. According to that verse, you could take your very best 1,000 days on this earth, put them together, and that would not equal just one day in God's presence in heaven. So, when times get tough, let's remain content because of that promise.

Comparison can get in the way of our pursuit of contentment. We'll discuss that more in the next chapter. Whatever is getting in the way, we have to do whatever it takes to fix the problem. As it says in 1 Timothy 6:6, "Godliness with contentment is great gain."

The question is, are we mainly living for this life or the next one? C. S. Lewis said, "If you read history you will find that the Christians that did the most for the present world are just the ones that thought the most of the next."[1] The only time we should not be content is when it comes to discipling others. I never want to be content with reaching others for Christ. If I'm really thinking about eternity, I will do everything I can to reach the lost in the short time I have here on earth. Charles Spurgeon said, "The Christian is the most contented man in the world, but the least contented WITH the world."[2] Let's be discontented with reaching the lost, but content in everything else.

I want to live like the man from Matthew 13. This man found an eternal treasure, and he knew exactly what to do with it. "The kingdom of heaven is like treasure hidden in a field. When a man found it, he hid it again, and then in his joy went and sold all he had and bought that field" (Matt. 13:44). This verse is comparing treasures on earth to treasures in heaven. And there's simply no comparison. When the man found this treasure, he instantly realized it was far greater than anything he had ever owned in his life. He realized that this treasure was worth losing everything else for. Our challenge is this: Do we treat heaven this way? Do we live our lives knowing that the treasure that awaits us is far greater than anything we could ever have here on earth?

Contentment is a choice, not a result. Joy is a choice, not a result. The Apostle Paul used the word *joy* 16 times in Philippians. He wrote that letter while in prison.

I won't always get everything I want in life. But my Father owns everything. I'm searching for Him all seven days of the week. And because of who He is, I lack nothing.

Chapter Eleven
Confidence and Comparison

One of my favorite movies growing up was *The Wizard of Oz*. It was made in 1939, so I think I'm safe giving some spoilers. There's a scene in the movie when Dorothy and her friends are standing before the Great and Powerful Oz for the very first time, and they're terrified. Who could blame them? They had heard of this wizard but didn't know for sure what he was like. As they're standing before him, there's a lot of smoke and fire. It's loud and frightening. The creepy wizard's face is up on the wall. Dorothy and her friends don't even know what to say or whether they're even allowed to approach him. One by one, they try to step forward to speak to this wizard, but all he does is yell at them and scare them away.

This is how a lot of people view God. Instead of seeing Him as a loving Father, they view God like He's this upset and unapproachable Being. They think He's sitting on His throne, but He doesn't want anyone to come near Him. And He just wants to yell at them for being so unworthy.

Scripture says otherwise. Hebrews 4:16 says, "Let us then approach God's throne of grace with confidence, so that we may receive mercy and find grace to help us in our time of need."

When we approach His throne, we can do it with confidence. We don't have to be afraid. We don't even have to worry about finding all the right words. Even when we are confessing sin, we can approach

Him with confidence because His throne is a throne of grace. First John 5:14 says, "This is the confidence we have in approaching God: that if we ask anything according to his will, he hears us." It's an incredible thing to trust that I can stand before my Maker knowing that He'll forgive me. As Thomas Watson said, "Christ went more willingly to the cross than we do to the throne of grace."[1]

The "Wizard of Oz" mentality of God needs to die, and Christians have a role to play in killing that view for good. As I previously stated, my basketball career took off when I found my confidence. That's been the case for many things in my life. I was never confident enough to approach a girl and ask her out unless I heard from somebody that she liked me. If I had that information, I went from shy kid to Backstreet Boy in seconds. I still remember how nervous I was when preaching the first few times, or singing, or starting out in my coaching career.

Caffeine has nothing on confidence. When we have confidence in who Christ is, it's a game changer. I no longer care as much about the approval of man when my confidence is in Jesus. I no longer have as much fear about the future when I'm confident in who holds it. Let these words speak to you, no matter what is currently going on in your life:

Being confident of this, that he who began a good work in you will carry it on to completion until the day of Christ Jesus.

—Phil. 1:6

"But blessed is the one who trusts in the LORD, whose confidence is in him."

—Jer. 17:7

In him and through faith in him we may approach God with freedom and confidence.

—Eph. 3:12

God is love. Whoever lives in love lives in God, and God in them. This is how love is made complete among us so that we will have confidence on the day of judgment: In this world we are like Jesus.

—1 John 4:16–17

And now, dear children, continue in Him, so that when He appears, we may be confident and unashamed before Him at His coming.

—1 John 2:28

The Comparison Game

Another benefit of having confidence in Christ is that we no longer need to compare ourselves to others. Have you ever played a game that you could never win? Maybe it was a video game or a game on your phone. Maybe it was playing one-on-one with an older sibling. Sometimes, we keep playing challenging games because there's at least a chance we can win. But if there was a game that you knew without a doubt you would lose, would you still play it?

Every single one of us does this when we play the comparison game. There's always going to be somebody better than you, even in the things you're good at. There's always going to be someone more popular than you, richer than you, more "successful" than you. It's easy to be content in life until you start comparing what you have to what other people have.

Comparison comes in many forms, and they're all equally dangerous. One form of comparison is when we compare our sin with other people's sin, and that's one of the worst games we can ever play. It's funny how we treat money at times, isn't it? You could take someone out to dinner and spend 50 bucks without blinking an eye. You can go to the movies and spend 25 bucks for the movie and overpriced popcorn. You could spend 100 bucks on a concert ticket or sporting event. But when the app you want on your phone costs

99 cents, you think, "Mmmm. I'm not really ready for that kind of commitment."

If you were buying a car, a few hundred bucks wouldn't make much of a difference in your final decision. But if a concert costs $300 instead of $100, you're probably not going. You reason, "I don't know if I can buy that $30 sweatshirt, but I'll easily spend that amount of money just to eat out tonight." I think we treat sin in a similar way. We pick and choose what sins are more "okay" than others. We compare our lives to others, and even though we are all sinners, we find ourselves thinking, "Yeah, but at least I don't struggle with *that* sin. I may struggle with pride or lust, but at least I don't struggle with drugs like that person over there." Jesus didn't go to a cross so we could fight over who is the better Christian.

This story in Luke 18 sums this point up nicely:

To some who were confident of their own righteousness and looked down on everyone else, Jesus told this parable: "Two men went up to the temple to pray, one a Pharisee and the other a tax collector. The Pharisee stood by himself and prayed: 'God, I thank you that I am not like other people—robbers, evildoers, adulterers—or even like this tax collector. I fast twice a week and give a tenth of all I get.'

"But the tax collector stood at a distance. He would not even look up to heaven, but beat his breast and said, 'God, have mercy on me, a sinner.' "I tell you that this man, rather than the other, went home justified before God. For all those who exalt themselves will be humbled, and those who humble themselves will be exalted."

—Luke 18:9–14

Are you confident in your own righteousness? Do you look down on others because of their sin? Or, do you say, "God, have mercy on me, a sinner"? We all need God's grace. We're all in process. I need the grace of God just as much as Hitler did.

Comparing what we have or don't have is also a horrible game to play. We are sometimes content with what we have until we see what someone else has. Social media is to blame for some of this. As Steven Furtick said, "One reason we struggle w/insecurity: we're comparing our behind the scenes to everyone else's highlight reel."[2] Why couldn't I get that job? Why can't I afford that kind of vacation? Why can't I get married like everybody else? Satan loves when we have these thoughts. Any time we keep our eyes on other people instead of Jesus, the powers of darkness rejoice.

By the grace of God, I've come a long way with this, but I used to compare myself to other people way too much. I would compare myself to people I went to Bible college with. I would have awful thoughts in my mind like, "How did that person get that job at that huge church? They must know someone who works there." When I left my job in Florida, I would drive myself crazy on social media seeing what the "new" youth pastor was doing with "my" students. I couldn't stop the comparison game. What a horrible way to live.

Sometimes, we even do this with the success people have! Instead of celebrating their accomplishments, we throw on a fake smile and continue to live in the bondage of jealousy.

Mike Donehey, the lead singer of Tenth Avenue North, asked, "What would it be like, if the people of God didn't care who God used, as long as He moved? I think rivers of joy would open before us."[3] Donehey also shared this thought: "Imagine if we didn't even need to be used by God? What if we were just as stoked when God used someone else?"[4]

We've got to start celebrating wins instead of worrying about comparison. That includes churches that get jealous at the success of the other church down the street. That's no way to build the Kingdom. Like Craig Groeschel says, "Comparison will either make you feel superior or inferior. Neither honors God."[5]

I worked in a lumberyard one summer when I was in college. The very first day I arrived, they told me I was going to work with another guy on the roof. It wasn't a flat roof, and I'm not a huge fan of heights. I love roller coasters and I'm perfectly fine on an airplane. When I feel like I could fall and die, however, I'm not a fan of heights. As soon as I got up on this roof, I knew I wouldn't be able to do it. But I also couldn't get down because it was difficult getting back on the ladder as I stared at my pending death over the ledge. They had to bring over a forklift truck so I could get on to be lowered down to the ground! Talk about embarrassing. Picture 30 dudes in a lumberyard watching a college student being lowered from a roof on a forklift!

At the time, though, I wasn't that embarrassed. I just wanted to live. In that moment, I didn't care what other people thought. In my life, I want to fear God and not what other people think. Even if I look stupid. Even if other people laugh at me. I just want to live the life God has for me. Who cares what other people think? In Galatians 1:10, Paul asks the key question: "Am I now trying to win the approval of human beings, or of God? Or am I trying to please people? If I were still trying to please people, I would not be a servant of Christ."

In John 21, Jesus was telling Peter the kind of death Peter would face as a result of following Jesus. Look at the conversation that took place as a result: "Peter turned and saw that the disciple whom Jesus loved was following them. . . . When Peter saw him, he asked, 'Lord, what about him?' Jesus answered, 'If I want him to remain alive until I return, what is that to you? You must follow me'" (John 21:20–22).

Peter was basically saying, "Why do I have to die? What about this guy?" And Jesus responded by saying, "What is his life to you? You follow me."

I'm not saying you will have to die for your faith. What I'm saying is we all have a different calling. It's a waste of time to compare our lives to other people. What God has for someone else shouldn't be our concern. Let's just focus on what He has in store for our own lives. He's the potter. I'm the clay. Make me and mold me however you want, God.

> *Let's just go ahead and be what we were made to be, without enviously or pridefully comparing ourselves with each other, or trying to be something we aren't.*
>
> —Rom. 12:6 MSG

I can't search for God with my full heart if I'm only looking at other people.

Chapter Twelve
Faith Like a Child

When I was a kid, I didn't ever want to leave home. I would often ask my parents, "Do I have to do anything today?" I think the biggest reason was because I had a big imagination. Give me a plastic Cubs helmet, a bat, and a few balls, and I could go play an entire game by myself in the backyard. Sometimes, I would even fake an injury in my pretend game, which didn't fly too well with my mother when she happened to be looking out the window. I was never bored because I always had my imagination.

Growing up in church, I was always told to have a "childlike faith." What does that look like? I think keeping or rediscovering our imagination is a good start. I don't play baseball by myself in the backyard anymore, but I still like to dream. I still use my imagination to do ministry and to enjoy life. You're never too young or too old to chase your dreams, no matter how big they may be.

Another way to have faith like a child is by being fully dependent on God. Kids are fully dependent on their parents for everything. A child needs their parents at all times just to keep them alive. And this is a beautiful picture of what it means to have faith like a child. We need to live our lives in this way. I want to be so close to my Creator that I need Him just as much as I need my next breath. He's the one who gave me breath in the first place, and I want to live a life that shows that. I don't want to just come to Him when I need something.

Later in life, kids may come to their parents only when they need something, but it didn't start out that way. Even though I can take care of myself now, I'm still fully dependent on God whether I live that way or not. Acknowledging my need for Him would make the whole process much easier.

As a child, I never felt scared on the road in a winter storm because I believed my dad was the best driver in the world. I always felt safe. During a storm, my mom would stay calm, which kept my sister and me calm. I always felt safe in their arms and in their presence. I depended on them. I never want to lose that dependence or safe feeling in the arms of my Heavenly Father.

I also want to laugh and ask questions like a child. Laughter is great medicine for us, not just physically but also spiritually. Psalm 126:2 says, "Our mouths were filled with laughter, our tongues with songs of joy. Then it was said among the nations, 'The LORD has done great things for them.'" It's estimated that children laugh between 200 and 300 times per day, while the average adult laughs 8 to 15 times per day. Why don't we laugh more? There's nothing better than hearing the laugh of a child, and I believe God never stops feeling that way about us. No matter how old we get, we are still a child in the eyes of God, and He's given us laughter and delights when we do so.

We should also never stop asking questions. On average, children between the ages of three and nine ask 300 questions per day. I'm not saying we should ask the "same" questions as children, but we should never lose our ability to ask questions in our lives. When we stop asking questions, we start feeling like we already have all the answers. One of my goals as a youth pastor is to help our students learn how to ask questions and to help them understand that asking them is a good thing, not a bad thing. If I just give them a bunch of answers all the time, then they never learn how to think for themselves. Not only that, but when we are having conversations about God with nonbelievers, the most effective thing we can do is ask the right questions to make them think instead of trying to spoon-feed them a bunch of statements. Over time, our questions should change as we learn and grow, but we should always have questions if we are to have faith like a child. The Bible is full of great questions: Paul's letter to the Romans is built around a series of questions. The first chapter of Hebrews begins and ends with questions. Jesus said to ask and it will be given to you. When the disciples asked Jesus questions about the parables He taught, He told them they had found the secret to the Kingdom. Look at the Psalms. They are filled with questions to God. When we have questions, we will seek the truth, and that's why we should never stop asking and seeking.

Humility is another key to a childlike faith. In Matthew 18:3–4, Jesus said, "Truly I tell you, unless you change and become like little children, you will never enter the kingdom of heaven. Therefore, whoever takes the lowly position of this child is the greatest in the kingdom of heaven."

On a scale of one to 10, how humble are you? Yes, that's a trick question. I think the correct answer is five, but I might be too proud of that answer.

Scripture is packed full of verses that teach us to be humble, but oftentimes as we get older, we tend to credit ourselves with the things we have accomplished. We tend to think we deserve the good things we have in life because we've worked hard to get them. And a lot of times by doing that, we lose the ability that we once had as children to fully appreciate all the blessings we have in our lives.

I want us to notice a pretty cool correlation between Scripture and a common theme among children. Most of the time, kids will receive more grace than adults when they do something they're not supposed to do. The main reason is because they're kids. People know they need to be shown extra grace so they can learn from their mistakes and because they don't always know the difference between good choices and bad choices. The Bible says, "God opposes the proud but gives grace to the humble" (James 4:6 ESV). So, think about that: children receive more grace when they do something wrong. A big reason for that is because children, for the most part, are very humble. I think there is a direct correlation here: if we are humble like a child, we will be given grace like a child. C. S. Lewis said, "Humility is not thinking less of yourself, but thinking of yourself less."[1]

Being humble is tough. We live in a world that teaches us to keep score. How many likes can you get? How many followers? Our politicians parade around talking about how great they are. This is completely opposite of how children think and what Jesus taught.

Consider this parable that Jesus taught:

> When someone invites you to a wedding feast, do not take the place of honor, for a person more distinguished than you may have been invited. If so, the host who invited both of you will come and say to you, "Give this person your seat." Then, humiliated, you will have to take the least important place. But when you are invited, take the lowest place, so that when your host comes, he will say to you, "Friend, move up to a better place." Then you will be honored in the presence of all the other guests. For all those who exalt themselves will be humbled, and those who humble themselves will be exalted.
>
> —Luke 14:8–11

During the time of this parable, every seat at a wedding was designated for a specific person. And if you were to sit in a seat higher than what you should have, you would be humiliated when asked to go to a lower seat. It would basically be like someone telling you, "You aren't as close to me as you thought." Or, "I don't like you **that** much!" It would be a terrible experience. But Jesus is teaching us that we should be humble. We should put others first and think of others before we think of ourselves.

And here's the challenge: Don't think of this story just in terms of events that you attend. Think of this story every day of your life. If I'm going to search for God every day, I need to ask this question every day: "How can I take the lowest seat today?" Imagine taking a lower seat at a banquet and having the master tell you, "Why are you sitting in this seat? I have a much better place for you." Now that would be a great feeling. Being humble is another way to keep our childlike faith.

To have faith like a child, I need to know I'm loved like a child. I'm loved by God in ways I can't even comprehend. My identity is "child of God." Nothing more. Nothing less.

I belong to my Abba. I depend on Him fully. He's big enough for my questions. Let's learn to dream again.

Chapter Thirteen

A Sense of Wonder

When I was growing up, my family and I would go to one Cubs game each summer. It was always my favorite day of the year no matter how good or bad the team was. Wrigley Field is still a magical place to me. Wrigley Field is located on Addison Street in Chicago. Naturally, I named my first child Addison.

When we went to the games, my mom wanted to see my facial expression when I first walked into Wrigley Field. So, after we walked in the gates with our tickets, my mom insisted on being the first one up the steps before we entered the ballpark so she could see my reaction. I would walk up the steps, look around, and I would just be amazed.

I want that kind of wonder and amazement in my relationship with God. I want to be mesmerized by Him. I want my time with God to be my favorite thing—something I always look forward to. I still get those feelings when I walk into Wrigley Field, and I never want to lose that sense of wonder with God either.

For you, it could be something entirely different than a baseball stadium. But think about that today: What in your life gives you that sense of excitement and wonder still to this day? Think back to your childhood or think about little kids and how their faces light up when they see certain things or go to certain places. Addison likes to find the moon at night when she's outside. When she finds it, you can just see the wonder in her eyes. Think about when a kid goes to Disney World or goes on vacation and sees the ocean or mountains for the very first time. Think about the things that make you feel the most alive and give you the greatest sense of awe and wonder. Now ask yourself: Do I get like that with my Creator?

Paul said this in Romans 1:20: "For since the creation of the world God's invisible qualities—his eternal power and divine nature—have been clearly seen, being understood from what has been made, so that people are without excuse." Then in verse 25 of Romans 1, Paul says, "They exchanged the truth about God for a lie, and worshiped and served created things rather than the Creator—who is forever praised. Amen."

Paul is saying that we can see God all around us. There's proof of Him through all creation, and all men are without excuse. He's also saying we cannot worship created things instead of the Creator. So when you do something you enjoy, such as going to a concert, enjoying food that you like, going to a sporting event, taking a vacation, or partaking even in the smaller joys of life, let it bring you into worship of your Creator, not the created thing itself.

Speaking of concerts, that's one of my favorite things to do. I really feel that sense of wonder of God when I'm experiencing live music and the communal experience of the crowd and the artist. I'll tell you one thing that drives me nuts is when people get out their phones and record an entire concert. I record a few parts of the show, but I try to make it minimal, and I try to get the shot, and then still look above my phone so I'm still present. If you're looking at the concert through your phone, why are you even there? I remember going to one concert when a lady in front of me recorded the entire thing, and she was looking directly into her screen the whole time. I wanted to say, "Lady, you're missing a great show up here!" You can get on YouTube and watch bad quality videos of live concerts any time you want. Our society is so obsessed with capturing things so they can see them later, or so they can post the video or photo online. It seems like we keep getting worse at living in the moment. I want to live in the here and now, and I want to be present. If I can do that more in my life, that's going to translate into my relationship with God. I want even the little joys of life to bring me into worship of my Creator.

Brennan Manning shared a story in his book *The Ragamuffin Gospel*. As the story goes, a rabbi was dying and he was asked, "What's the greatest thing you think God gave you in your life?" He could've said anything in that moment, but he said, "He gave me a sense of wonder. Never once in my life did I ask for success, or power, or fame. I asked for wonder, and He gave it to me."[1] What a great example to follow. As a father, youth pastor, coach, and a human, one of the top goals in my life is to be present, enjoy every moment, and be amazed by God's creation and every blessing He's given to me. I'm not a morning person, but Scripture tells me His mercies are new every morning. So let's drink some coffee and reflect on God's mercies, and that will help us get our mind in the right place for the day.

One of the greatest joys I've ever had in my life is when my two-year-old daughter sees me from across the hall and yells "Daddy! Daddy!" and sprints in my direction to give me a hug. It's hard to even describe how that feels. Other times, it can be crushing when she doesn't want her daddy and wants someone or something else. But do I love her any less in those times? Absolutely not. My love for her will never change, no matter what she does. God loves us even when we choose other people or other things instead of Him. His love for us will never change. But I know it brings Him incredible joy when we say "Abba" (Daddy) and run into His arms. That's how I want to live.

I'm also reminded that God said these words to Moses, "Take off your sandals, for the place you are standing is holy ground" (Exod. 3:5). I don't know what places feel the most like holy ground to you. Outside of the Wrigley Field example, I've been on several mission trips or vacations that gave me those thoughts.

In college, I took a mission trip to Hawaii. That's really roughing it, right? Hey, people in Hawaii need Jesus too! We served with a homeless organization called Feed My Sheep. Maui has a large homeless population for multiple reasons. We also helped clear out a jungle area so a lady could use the land to put on Christian retreats for kids. We also got to experience Maui. One of my friends has an uncle who lived there, and he was basically our tour guide. It was an unbelievable experience.

I've also been to New Orleans and New England for mission trips. It's great to see what God is doing in other parts of the country. It's also great to see His creation and His beauty in different places. My wife and I also visit a new city every year, which is something I highly encourage for everyone who is able to make it happen. We've been to Nashville, Boston, Philadelphia, and Toronto, to name a few. These mountaintop experiences are needed. They can feed our soul. They can make us feel alive. By all means, go to the places that make you feel closest to God.

But I remember having a thought when we would get back home from these amazing trips; I would look at a beautiful sunset in the small town where I live and think, "You know what? This is holy ground too!" Sometimes, we think holy ground is just in a place like Israel, or it's just in Hawaii, or it's just at the ocean, or out in nature. Those places are good for us for sure. Those places can help bring us closer to God. But the ground we are standing on right now is holy ground too.

There's a reason Jesus would go out in nature all the time. He'd go to pray. He would go to get His mind right, and He'd go to enjoy time with His Father. Right before His ministry began, He spent 40 days in the wilderness. We need moments like that too. But it's not just about the times we get away from everything. It's also about the day-to-day moments.

From time to time, take off your sandals, for you are standing on holy ground.

Sometimes, we feel like God is distant, or not even there at all. The truth is, He's never the one who is lost. We are. Think about when you lose something, like your car keys or your jacket or your wallet. Usually, the item isn't really lost; we just can't remember where we put it. The item isn't lost. We are. When God feels distant in our lives, could it be the same thing? The truth is God is always with us. What we need is more awareness of His presence.

It's easy to have a great experience with God at a camp, conference, church service, or concert. What about when you get home? God is the same God from camp, and He's here. May we be aware of His presence every day.

Instead of saying, "God be with us" or "God please show up in this situation," I want to say, "God help us be aware of your presence." He's always present. Sometimes, we lack awareness that He's present.

A. W. Tozer has some amazing quotes on this topic. He said, "It is exactly as near to God from any place as it is from any other place. A man is not nearer to Christ on Easter Sunday than he is any other day. As long as Christ sits on the throne, every day is a good day and all days are days of salvation."[2] Tozer also said: "Private prayer, Bible meditation, church attendance, service—all should be engaged by every Christian. But at the bottom of all these things, giving meaning to them, will be the inward habit of beholding God."[3]

Think about the early church in the book of Acts. They didn't do all those amazing things just because Peter and Paul preached a great sermon series. The first Christians were very aware of God's presence wherever they went. They knew He was at work in all things. They knew that because of what Jesus had done God was no longer confined to a building or a certain place. He was everywhere and at work in all things. They marveled at that.

I never want to have a reaction like Jacob did in Genesis 28:16: "When Jacob awoke from his sleep, he thought, "Surely the LORD is in this place, and I was not aware of it." As A. W. Tozer once said, "Men do not know God is here. What a difference it would make if they knew!"[4]

Scripture also says, "The fear of the LORD is the beginning of wisdom" (Ps. 111:10). When the Bible talks about fearing the Lord, I don't believe it's talking about being afraid of God. What I've learned is that fearing the Lord means to be in awe of Him. So, in that verse, you could basically say, "Being in awe of God is the beginning of wisdom."

When we live our lives in awe of Him, it changes our perspective on everything else. One thing that upsets me is when people try to pin science and faith up against each other, or when people say it's a battle of the Bible vs. Science. There are people who say, "I don't believe in God because of science." I believe that how Christians have treated the topic of science is one reason people have made science and faith some kind of competition. The truth is Christians sometimes come across as ignorant or close-minded when it comes to things like science. When in reality, Christians should be the most curious people on the planet. We should look at new scientific discoveries, and say: "Oh, that's what God did there," instead of being totally closed off to different possibilities. I love hearing about science, and even when someone claims something is true that I may disagree with, I can still approach the situation and learn something, and be even more in awe of God with what I'm learning.

Ravi Zacharias says, "Our sense of wonder is a blessing from God, given so that we would be continually amazed at His beauty and creation."[5] Christians should be the biggest dreamers on the planet. We should be the ones asking the most questions. We should want to go after truth and make new discoveries. I want to discover new things about God and His creation on a daily basis. I want to say "How" and "Wow" all the time. A lot of unbelievers think the Christian's only response is, "The Bible says this, and the Bible says that." The Bible is where we find Total Truth. It's the source of our lives. It's how we view everything else. But it's not the only way God speaks. How did God speak to the people of the Bible? With the Bible? No! He spoke to them in multiple ways. Saying "God only speaks through Scripture" is simply not true. He speaks through nature, through other people, through pain, through our dreams, through our desires, and through the prompting of the Holy Spirit. Let our lives be filled with awe and wonder of the very God who made us and everything we see.

Here's another good quote to live by from Mary Oliver: "Pay attention. Be astonished. Tell someone about it."[6] I want to look at God the same way my 10-year-old self looked walking into Wrigley Field. I want to be a dreamer. I want to ask questions. I want to live every day with gratitude and in awe of my Maker. I want to be aware of His presence because I know He's already here. Because of what Jesus Christ did on the cross and because He rose from the dead I have an entirely new perspective on life and my future and my destiny.

Take off your sandals, for you are standing on holy ground.

Chapter Fourteen
No Pain, No Gain

In 2005, a little girl named Gabby Gingras went on *The Oprah Winfrey Show* with her family. Gabby had a rare health condition that didn't allow her to feel pain of any kind. While that may sound like a good thing, it was actually a nightmare. When we don't feel any pain, we don't know there's a problem. We don't know how to get better, or to ask for help. Her mother said, "My greatest prayer is that my daughter could feel pain."[1]

Pain is a necessary part of growth. Pain isn't fun, but it's important. Pain is often the very thing that causes us to turn to God. If we never experienced any pain in our lives, would we have any need for our Heavenly Father? Would we even search for Him at all?

If you've ever been told the Christian life would be easy, you were lied to. One day, there will be no more pain. But while we still live on this broken and sinful planet, there will be pain.

Our very Savior faced unimaginable pain. Why would we assume life would be easy for us? The half brother of Jesus said this:

Consider it pure joy, my brothers and sisters, whenever you face trials of many kinds, because you know that the testing of your faith produces perseverance. Let perseverance finish its work so that you may be mature and complete, not lacking anything.

—James 1:2–4

He doesn't just say we'll face pain. He says we should consider it pure joy because of what it will produce in our lives.

How about a best friend of Jesus? Peter said this: "Therefore, since Christ suffered in his body, arm yourselves also with the same attitude, because whoever suffers in the body is done with sin" (1 Pet. 4:1). Then, he said, "If you suffer as a Christian, do not be ashamed, but praise God that you bear that name" (1 Pet. 4:16).

Whether it's persecution from nonbelievers or some kind of tragedy that we face, we will all experience pain and suffering in this life. When those things happen, will we turn to God or away from Him? Will we keep searching for Him in those moments or turn our backs?

I haven't heard many stories from people saying, "My life was perfect, so I decided to turn my life over to Jesus." Usually, the story is more like this: "I lost everything. My life was broken. I knew I needed a change, and I experienced a closeness to God like never before."

My friend's aunt passed away at a young age from cancer. It was tragic. But through her death, her husband came to know Jesus. We may face physical pain if it means spiritual healing is needed. MercyMe's lead singer Bart Millard said the best thing that ever happened to his dad was getting cancer. It brought them together.[2] It brought his dad to Jesus. Years later, Bart is reaching millions of people with that amazing testimony. This doesn't mean we'll always have answers for our pain. And it doesn't mean it will ever get easier. But we have to try to understand that pain is sometimes a necessary part of our lives.

Sometimes, we experience pain as a consequence of our actions. Other times, it has nothing to do with anything we've done. If you're ever tempted to ask why bad things happen to good people, remember this response by R. C. Sproul: "That only happened once, and He volunteered for it."[3]

Never forget that "Jesus wept" (John 11:35). He knew He was going to raise Lazarus from the dead, but He still experienced great pain in the moment for His friends. Later, His mother, Mary, felt incredible pain standing before the cross even though she had confidence her son would return in a few days. Even when we're confident in how the story ends, pain is still part of the journey. We shouldn't bottle it up or ignore it. It's okay to cry out to God.

If you struggle with mental health, depression, or suicidal thoughts, you are no less of a person and no less of a Christian than anyone else. Sometimes, our pain can't even be explained or articulated fully, but it's still there. Thankfully, we're never alone in our pain. Scripture is filled with men and women who had major struggles even as they walked closely with God. Jonah was trying to end his life before being swallowed by a big fish; he wasn't just going for a fun little swim. Moses and Elijah both asked God to end their lives. David and other Psalmists shouted their questions, doubts, and fears. If a Christian tells you that you shouldn't have doubts or questions, you've been lied to. God can handle our issues, and He's with us in our pain.

As a basketball coach, I don't enjoy disciplining my teams or making them run. Conditioning isn't the fun part of the game. But the pain is necessary for growth. Being too tired in the fourth quarter and losing is much more painful than running in practice to prepare for battle. I believe in the "No pain, No gain" slogan in sports. And now, I believe it for my life and my faith as well.

"How could God be loving if He allows children to starve or get killed?" "How can you believe in a God at all with such pain in the world?" There are no easy answers to these questions. But I do know God's Word predicts evil and tragedy in this life. We live in a fallen, sinful, broken world. Pain is inevitable on this earth. If there was nothing more than this life, I would also question God's love and why so many bad things happen. But I believe there's more. I believe eternity awaits, and this temporary life won't even come close to measuring up. Even though it's hard, we've got to try to have that eternal perspective instead of living as if this world is all we have.

Psalm 34:18 says, "The LORD is close to the brokenhearted and saves those who are crushed in spirit." According to this, you could even argue we are better off when we're going through pain. Being near to God is always a great place to be. The Lord is always near, but we might be more aware of it when we're dealing with a broken heart.

In my search for God, I know that growth won't happen from comfort. We've got to work for the things we want. As Zig Ziglar said, "There is no elevator to success. You have to take the stairs."[4] Climbing the mountain won't be easy, but the struggle on the way up will make reaching the top much more meaningful.

When surfer Bethany Hamilton lost her arm in a shark attack, she wanted to get right back in the water within weeks. She knew it wouldn't be easy to surf with one arm, but she said, "I don't need easy. I just need possible."[5] Too many Christians are looking for the safe, comfortable, and painless life. It doesn't exist. Pain is temporary, but so is happiness. Your circumstances can change in a second.

I have a confession to make: I'm a sportsaholic. Sports have not only given me an incredible amount of joy in my life, but they've also taught me many life lessons. The number one thing sports have taught me is that we should never be too high or too low in our lives. When things are going well in sports and in life, stay humble. Things can change in a hurry. When things are going poorly in life, stay faithful. Again, things can change in a hurry. Sports have helped me to be even-keeled and calm even in the craziest of situations.

When we go through pain, stay the course. Keep pressing on. Better days are ahead. Maybe the current pain is there to draw us closer to God. Maybe it's there so we can help others with the same pain in the future. Maybe it's the only way we can grow.

God can handle our questions. We can shout at Him at the top of our lungs, and He'll listen to every word. He understands our frustrations. Instead of hiding our pain, bring it before God. I love what Jon Foreman said about the story of Jacob: "Jacob wrestled with God. From that day on, he walked with a limp. In a lot of ways, I don't trust a man who doesn't have a limp."[6]

I want my faith to grow, even if it takes pain to get there. I want to walk with a limp. I want people to see a faith that is real, seven days a week. Pain is inevitable—how we respond is the question.

"When the burden seems too much to bear, remember: the end will justify the pain it took to get us there."

—Relient K

Chapter Fifteen

Will Call

I didn't find my "career" calling until I was a senior in college. But I found my "daily" calling much earlier than that. There is a big difference between the two.

One of the top questions I get asked is, "How do I know what my calling is? How do I know what God's will is?" God's will for your life is more of a journey than a destination. It's way more about following Him daily than about your future career. I agree fully with this saying: "Your calling is where your feet are." *Relevant* magazine put it like this: "God's will is not a mystery to be solved, but a road to be traveled."[1]

You may not find out what you were meant to do for a career until much later in life, and that calling could even change several times. The Bible isn't going to tell you, "Bobby, you are called to be a teacher." But it will tell you many things about what God is calling you to do right now. This very day. Here are a few examples:

Rejoice always, pray continually, give thanks in all circumstances; for this is God's will for you in Christ Jesus.

—1 Thess. 5:16–18

Do not conform to the pattern of this world, but be transformed by the renewing of your mind. Then you will be able to test and approve what God's will is—his good, pleasing and perfect will.

—Rom. 12:2

For it is God's will that by doing good you should silence the ignorant talk of foolish people.

—1 Pet. 2:15

Look carefully then how you walk, not as unwise but as wise, making the best use of the time, because the days are evil. Therefore do not be foolish, but understand what the will of the Lord is.

—Ephesians 5:15–17 ESV

What is God's will for your life? He wants you to give thanks in all circumstances, transform your mind, live in a way that silences the doubters, and make the most of every opportunity you are given. It's also clear from Scripture that He wants us to be His witnesses "to the ends of the earth" (Acts 1:8). And the greatest commands are to "Love God, and love people." None of these things have anything to do with a college degree, future plans, or a career choice. Maybe one day God will call you to the mission field, but I can promise you He's calling you to do mission work where you live right now. Maybe one day God will put someone in your life to marry. In the meantime, He's calling you to honor him while being single.

Jon Foreman was asked about calling, and this is what he had to say:

Calling has this weight that somehow we think that your calling is fixed, or that your calling is this line that you've finally found and now you're on that track and that's what you're going to do forever. But I feel like calling has much more to do with the moment that you're in. If you happen to be right there when a car accident happened, your calling is to make sure that everyone's okay. If you are next to your friend when she finds out her mom died, your calling is to be there for her and comfort her. When I was in my twenties, calling meant one thing: it meant writing songs about my roommates in college. And now, it means something different. But I think the idea of calling is not a permanent thing. It's got to change from time to time.[2]

What does this look like in your life right now? Are your eyes open to the needs around you? Are you attacking each day with purpose? Or are you more focused on what you will do later in life? Some of the best advice I've ever received is to make your dreams big but make your steps small. We should think big and pursue what God's ultimate calling is for our lives, but being faithful in the smaller things of life is the way we eventually get there.

I'm blown away by the number of people that would give up some of their lives just so they could get to the next thing in life. At one of our youth group meetings in February, I asked the students, "How many of you would skip to summer right now if you could?" About 75 percent of them raised their hands. So, I asked them, "Are you telling me that you would willingly give up three months of your life just so you could get to summer break?" When it's Monday, would you give up five days of your life just to get to the weekend? When you're 14, would you give up two years of your life just to get your driver's license? We're never going to live out our daily calling if we're more concerned about the future than the present. Even when you're going through a rough time in life, don't wish it away. You have a purpose today.

The truth is, the Bible doesn't really talk about tomorrow except to say, "Don't worry about tomorrow" (Matt. 6:34 NLT) or "Do not boast about tomorrow" (Prov. 27:1). It's all about today. Martin Luther said, "I have two days in my calendar: This day, and *that day*."[3] That's a great way to live. We can still plan for the future, but our mindset should be on today, and the day Christ returns. Those are the only two days that really matter for me right now. As Joshua said, "Choose for yourselves this day whom you will serve. . . . But as for me and my household, we will serve the LORD" (Josh. 24:15).

Choosing to follow Jesus isn't a one-time thing at a powerful night at camp. We have to choose Him *this* very day, over and over again.

When Jesus said to Matthew, "Follow me," imagine if Matthew had said: "Okay, Jesus, I'll follow you, but could you tell me where I'll be five years from now? What's the big picture here, Lord? What does this mean for my life in the future?" Instead of saying that, Matthew just dropped everything and followed Him. That's what our daily lives should look like. Where is Jesus calling me today? What does Jesus want me to do today? Who needs the gospel today? That's got to be our focus.

I love what David Platt has to say about our calling in his book *Radical*. He says:

> I find it interesting that one of the most common questions asked today among Christians is "What is God's will for my life?" or "How do I find God's will for my life?" Many Christians have almost assumed the attitude that they would obey God if He would just show them what He wanted them to do. But in the middle of a Christian culture asking "How do I find God's will for my life," I bring good news: His will is not lost. With so many nonbelievers in the world, it makes little sense for us to sit here asking "What do you want me to do God?" . . . The answer is clear: the will of God is for you and me to give our lives urgently, and recklessly to making the gospel known among all people. The question, therefore, is not "Can we find God's Will?" The question is: "Will we obey God's Will?"[4]

One of the things I've been called to do is to coach basketball. One of the main messages I give to my players is to make the next play. If we're down by 20 points or up by 20 points, I'll often ask them, "What's the score?" If they don't say 0–0, I correct them. You have to treat the next quarter like the score is tied. I think God wants us to face each day with that mindset. There's no need to worry too much about the past or the future. Let's focus on the here and now.

One of the frustrations of coaching is when players just don't listen. You can draw a play up in a time-out, but they could still ignore what you told them 30 seconds later. I wonder how many times God has felt that way about me. Sometimes, I tell my players, "If you would just listen, things would work out." I bet God has had those thoughts about me many times in this life. If I would just listen to Him each day, I'd be a lot better off.

As for your future, I believe God will reveal His bigger plans for you in His timing, as long as you're following Him and listening. What makes you feel the most alive? What gives you purpose and meaning instead of just a paycheck? What is something you love so much that you'd do for free? Maybe that's your career calling.

Walt Disney said, "We don't make movies to make money. We make money to make more movies."[5] Not everyone will understand what you're called to do, and that shouldn't matter. The most successful people have the most critics.

I felt called to bring unity to the youth groups in my community, so I started a project called "Unite C'ville." We put together several events and invited all the local youth groups to join together for worship, entertainment, prayer, and service. Lots of youth groups were involved, and they loved it. Some decided not to attend, which was their loss. One youth group attended only one of the events. The youth pastor at that church wanted to meet with me the following week to "analyze" the event. He actually had his kids write down the positives and negatives of the event, instead of focusing on the spirit of unity, which was the whole point. He probably thought he was helping me with this information, but it was really just beating me down. All I wanted was for kids in the community to experience the joy of being unified with other believers. You know how it is. You can get 100 compliments, but you take the one criticism to heart. As Lecrae said in his book *Unashamed*, "There can be 10,000 adoring fans at my show, but the two people who trashed me online dominate my thoughts. The two don't matter. Neither do the 10,000. It only matters what the One thinks."[6]

A few months later, I found out that this very event saved someone's life. Literally. A student in my youth group invited one of her friends to this event, and this person was a few days away from taking his own life. This event that another youth pastor trashed was the very event that saved someone's soul. And now, this student is a strong Christian who loves to do ministry.

If you feel called to do something, do it. Let the critics talk all they want. Stay focused on the prize. Run your race. As Rich Mullins once said, "David didn't kill Goliath because he set out to slay giants. He set out to give sandwiches to his brothers, and Goliath got in the way."[7]

Your calling is where your feet are. So, bloom wherever you are planted.

Chapter Sixteen

Whatevers and Weirdos

When I played basketball at Lincoln Christian University, it was really interesting to see how our opponents and their fans treated us. Less than half of our games were against other Christian colleges, so the bulk of our schedule was against secular schools. Sometimes, the opposition had a lot of respect for us. Other times, not so much. One night, my teammate set a hard screen and it knocked an opposing player to the ground. He stood up and said, "I thought you guys were a Christian school!" And he wasn't kidding.

What was this guy expecting? Should we just hand him the ball and say, "Bless you, my child, here's the basketball. Since we are Christians, we will allow you to score on us at your convenience." No way. I would understand questioning our faith if we were cussing at the opposition or playing dirty. But setting a good hard screen is just playing the game. Are we supposed to be weak and not play hard because we are Christians? I would suggest doing the complete opposite.

In Colossians 3, we are told some very important instructions:

And whatever you do, whether in word or deed, do it all in the name of the Lord Jesus, giving thanks to God the Father through him.

—Col. 3:17

Then a few verses later:

"Whatever you do, work at it with all your heart, as working for the Lord not for human masters."

—Col. 3:23

Whatever I'm doing, I'm supposed to give it all I've got. Not for the approval of others, but to please my Maker. Even playing a game of basketball. Even doing a homework assignment. Even while I'm at work. I believe it pleases God when I give my best in all things. If you're playing a game and your team is down by 30 points, does it please God if you keep your head up and continue to play hard? I believe it does. Does it please God when you have to do something for work, and you give it all you've got even if nobody else even notices? I believe it does. If you lead a church of 30 people or a church of 10,000, your job is to give it all you've got and pursue excellence. We each have an audience of One.

It used to be cool to say "Whatever" as a response to just about anything. Maybe some of the "cool kids" still use this expression. Let's think of the word with a new perspective. Whatever I do, I can use it as worship. Whatever I do, I can please God with my effort. Paul liked the word *whatever*. In his letter to the Philippians, he said these famous words:

Finally, brothers and sisters, whatever is true, whatever is noble, whatever is right, whatever is pure, whatever is lovely, whatever is admirable—if anything is excellent or praiseworthy—think about such things. Whatever you have learned or received or heard from me, or seen in me—put it into practice. And the God of peace will be with you.

—Phil. 4:8–9

We are called to set our minds and our focus on "whatever" is true, noble, right, pure, lovely, admirable, and praiseworthy. That's a pretty big list.

Jesus liked this word too. In Matthew's Gospel, He said, "Truly I tell you, whatever you did for one of the least of these brothers and sisters of mine, you did for me'" (Matt. 25:40). Maybe we could ask these questions each day: What am I doing today? I will use it as worship. What do I have today? I will share it with who needs it.

I'm fascinated with the number seven. Can you tell? The number seven represents "completion" in Scripture. It's identified with things being "finished" or a "divine perfection." There were seven days represented in Creation. Animals were seven days old before being sacrificed. Joshua marched around Jericho for seven days. We see seven signs in John's Gospel, seven things the Lord hates in Proverbs 6, seven parables in Matthew 13, seven woes in Matthew 23, and Jesus's seven "I AM" statements in John. This number is used in the Bible over 700 times. The number seven is the number of God. I'm searching for seven in my life. One of the best ways to do that is by searching for Him in whatever I'm doing. I want to treat even the mundane and small things of life with an awareness of God as I seek to find Him in all things.

I want to go wherever He wants me to go, and I want to do whatever He tells me to do. Luke records one of my favorite stories in all of Scripture. Imagine being a professional fisherman and then being told how to fish by someone else:

When he had finished speaking, he said to Simon, "Put out into deep water, and let down the nets for a catch." Simon answered, "Master, we've worked hard all night and haven't caught anything. But because you say so, I will let down the nets." When they had done so, they caught such a large number of fish that their nets began to break. So they signaled their partners in the other boat to come and help them, and they came and filled both boats so full that they began to sink.

—Luke 5:4–7

Whenever I question what God wants me to do, I want to have the attitude of Simon from this story. You want me to forgive that person? I'd rather not, but because You say so, I will. You want me to give how much to the offering? Because you say so, I will. You want me to make major changes in my life? Because you say so, I will.

We're the Weirdos

If I'm truly going to worship God in whatever I do, I'm going to come across as being weird at times—and that's a good thing. A. W. Tozer said, "Go to church once a week and nobody pays attention. Worship God seven days a week and you become strange!"[1]

I don't want to be weird in the cheesy, judgmental, or ignorant kind of ways. I want to be weird in the servant-minded, forgiving, and genuine kind of ways. I was listening to Christian radio while driving one day, so that was my fault. A lady started talking in between songs, and I want you to imagine the cheesiest voice you've ever heard saying this: "The other day I was trying to type the word *God* on my computer, but it kept autocorrecting and spelling it *good* instead. And then I thought to myself, God *is* good!"

I felt like pulling the car over so I could throw up.

Nothing against this radio host—she had good intentions. But things like that just make me cringe. I can't imagine how a nonbeliever would feel if they happened to listen to it. Over-the-top cheesy is not a good thing. We've got to be real. Christians can come across as weird in a bad way. Let's talk about the bad kind versus the good.

- Bad weird – In sports, saying you won a game because "God was on your side." Really? Does God not like the other team? Did you pray harder than them?
- Good weird – Showing respect and sportsmanship during games.
- Bad weird – The people who didn't tip a waitress because she was gay. The post went viral, and Christians were mocked.
- Good weird – Giving someone a big tip despite poor service because you see they're having a rough night.

- Bad weird – Treating material possessions like life or death. Letting "stuff" ruin your day.
- Good weird – Having an eternal perspective. Someone hits your car or breaks something of yours, and you tell them: "Hey, it's okay. It's just stuff. It's fine."
- Bad weird – Judging everyone else's sin while ignoring your own.
- Good weird – Admitting your own mistakes and knowing we're all equally guilty.
- Bad weird – Pretending like we have all the answers.
- Good weird – Admitting we don't.

This list could go on and on. The point is this: we should live a life that demands explanation. I want people to look at my life and question why I'm so joyful, why I'm so forgiving, and why I have such a servant's heart.

Let's live out the spirit of this passage from 1 Peter and make it real:

Live such good lives among the pagans that, though they accuse you of doing wrong, they may see your good deeds and glorify God on the day he visits us. Submit yourselves for the Lord's sake to every human authority: whether to the emperor, as the supreme authority, or to governors, who are sent by him to punish those who do wrong and to commend those who do right. For it is God's will that by doing good you should silence the ignorant talk of foolish people.

—1 Pet. 2:12–15

If someone doesn't believe what you believe, let them see what you believe with your life. Make them think a little bit. Make them want what you have. After all, we're the aliens on this planet. Our citizenship is in heaven. We're going to be the weirdos at times, but let's be the good kind.

In whatever we do, let's worship.

Chapter Seventeen

Grace vs. Law

All loving parents have rules for their kids. Otherwise, they wouldn't be loving. Imagine if a parent told their child, "You're not allowed to play in the busy street," and the kid responded by saying, "You don't love me! If you loved me, you'd let me do whatever I want!" Ridiculous, right? Yet so many people treat the commands of God in a similar way. "Why would God have so many rules if He really loved us?"

The truth is that Christians today live in the New Covenant that Jesus introduced. We no longer live under the Law. We live under His grace. Even the 10 commandments were for the nation of Israel during a specific time in history, not a prerequisite for a 21st-century Christian's salvation.

Many people believe you have to follow God's commands, or you can't be a Christian. Or they believe God doesn't love you if you don't obey everything. This turns people away from the true gospel, because we're all aware of our imperfections. We have to ask ourselves this question: If I needed to follow all God's commands for Him to love me, why did Jesus go to the cross? What was the point of Him dying a brutal death if I could just follow some checklist and be good to go?

This life-changing verse is something we should never forget: "I do not set aside the grace of God, for if righteousness could be gained through the law, Christ died for nothing" (Gal. 2:21). If my righteousness could be attained by following God's laws, then Christ died for no reason. I'm searching for seven (perfection), but I can't possibly measure up. Nobody on this planet could score a 100 percent on this test, and that's the whole point.

These are two simple truths that we've either misunderstood or ignored:

God's commands are for our own good and bring freedom.
God's commands are meant to show us our need for a Savior.

In the famous "Prodigal Son" story, there are many truths to understand. One of them often gets overlooked. One son took the money and left town. He wanted to live his own life and didn't care about his family anymore. But after he lost everything due to a famine, he realized he made a mistake. Here's the rest of the story from Luke 15:

When he came to his senses, he said, "How many of my father's hired servants have food to spare, and here I am starving to death! I will set out and go back to my father and say to him: Father, I have sinned against heaven and against you. I am no longer worthy to be called your son; make me like one of your hired servants." So he got up and went to his father.

But while he was still a long way off, his father saw him and was filled with compassion for him; he ran to his son, threw his arms around him and kissed him.

The son said to him, "Father, I have sinned against heaven and against you. I am no longer worthy to be called your son."

But the father said to his servants, "Quick! Bring the best robe and put it on him. Put a ring on his finger and sandals on his feet. Bring the fattened calf and kill it. Let's have a feast and celebrate. For this son of mine was dead and is alive again; he was lost and is found." So they began to celebrate.

Meanwhile, the older son was in the field. When he came near the house, he heard music and dancing. So he called one of the servants and asked him what was going on. "Your brother has come," he replied, "and your father has killed the fattened calf because he has him back safe and sound."

The older brother became angry and refused to go in. So his father went out and pleaded with him. But he answered his father, "Look! All these years I've been slaving for you and never disobeyed your orders. Yet you never gave me even a young goat so I could celebrate with my friends. But when this son of yours who has squandered your property with prostitutes comes home, you kill the fattened calf for him!"

"My son," the father said, "you are always with me, and everything I have is yours. But we had to celebrate and be glad, because this brother of yours was dead and is alive again; he was lost and is found."

—Luke 15:17–32

Don't overlook this fact: the son realized it would be better to work for his Father than to live freely without Him. Do you ever feel tied down by God's commands? We are more free living in God's direction than choosing to live however we want without Him. Like everybody else, I sometimes wish certain things weren't in the Bible. I'd rather do my own thing at times. But I would just end up like the son in the story if I did. I may enjoy the freedom for a while, until I realized it wasn't freedom at all.

We don't live under the Old Testament Law anymore, but there's still a lot of principles to take from it. The Israelites were given the 10 commandments right after they were rescued from slavery. Think about that. They were rescued from slavery, and then given another set of rules to follow. Why? Because following God's ways is actually the ultimate freedom. Read through Psalm 119 sometime. David "delighted" in God's Law. Does that sound like someone who was tied down? I didn't always like the rules my parents had for me growing up, but I actually had more freedom later in life because I (mostly) obeyed them. Now consider that God is a perfect Heavenly Father. The One who made us knows what we need. There's freedom in following Him.

His commands are for our own good. They bring freedom. And they were also put in place to show us our need for a Savior in the first place. When we read Scripture about the sins we commit, we shouldn't read it as a condemnation. We should read it like a diagnosis. Charles Spurgeon said, "The point of contact between the patient and the Physician is the disease."[1] If we didn't know we were sick, why would we need a doctor? It's like God told us, "Here's a bunch of things to follow. It will be for your own good if you obey them. But I know you won't be able to. And since you can't, that's proof that you need a Savior. Here's Jesus."

If we want to share the true gospel message, we can't overlook these incredible verses:

Before it was possible to be saved from the punishment of sin by putting our trust in Christ, we were held under the Law. It was as if we were being kept in prison. We were kept this way until Christ came. The Law was used to lead us to Christ. It was our teacher, and so we were made right with God by putting our trust in Christ.

—Gal. 3:23–24 NLV

Well then, am I suggesting that the law of God is sinful? Of course not! In fact, it was the law that showed me my sin. I would never have known that coveting is wrong if the law had not said, "You must not covet."

—Rom. 7:7 NLT

The message of the gospel is not "behavior modification." I want to obey God because He saved me instead of obeying and hoping it's enough to get me saved. As Timothy Keller says, "The more you understand how your salvation isn't about your behavior, the more radically your behavior will change."[2]

I remember hearing a United States vice president say, "We need Jesus more than ever right now." I understand what he was trying to say, and I was glad a politician was mentioning Jesus, but I disagree with the statement. We need Jesus every minute of every day. We need Him just as much this very second as we need Him in a time of crisis. I need the grace of God just to write this very sentence and breathe this very breath. And the sooner I realize that, the sooner I'll understand just how amazing His grace is.

When I was really young, I remember my parents going to the "money-mover" (ATM) when they needed some extra cash for the day. When I would ask them for an expensive game or toy, they would occasionally say, "No, that's too expensive." I would say, "What do you mean? Just go get some money from the money-mover to pay for it!" I was too young to understand that the ATM is not a machine that gives away free money. It's obviously money you've put in your account, and it can run out. Some people live as if God's grace can run out in their lives. But His grace has no bounds. Unlike our money, His grace will never end. I'm thankful we are saved by His grace, and not by our own works.

That leads us to an interesting debate. If we are saved by grace and not by our own works, why does the Bible still teach us that we need to do good works? Why does it give us commands to follow? Is this a contradiction? I like to turn to John 15 to answer this question:

No branch can bear fruit by itself; it must remain in the vine. Neither can you bear fruit unless you remain in me. "I am the vine; you are the branches. If you remain in me and I in you, you will bear much fruit;

apart from me you can do nothing. If you do not remain in me, you are like a branch that is thrown away and withers; such branches are picked up, thrown into the fire and burned. If you remain in me and my words remain in you, ask whatever you wish, and it will be done for you. This is to my Father's glory, that you bear much fruit, showing yourselves to be my disciples."

—John 15:4–8

We're supposed to "bear much fruit" to show we're actually His disciples. But we can't do that on our own. We are like a tree branch, and He's the Vine. If we stay connected to the vine, we will naturally bear fruit. If we aren't connected to the Vine, we won't. Which means: if we aren't producing fruit in our lives, we aren't as connected to the Vine as we thought. Yes, we are saved by grace. But if there's no evidence of our faith in Christ, it probably means we don't really know Him. Get connected to the Vine, and the fruit will follow. The fruit of the Spirit will be evidence that our relationship with Jesus is real.

I Like Big Buts

I like this section, and I cannot lie. I'm convinced that the Bible has the best but(s) in the world. Look at the first part of Romans 6:23: "For the wages of sin is death." Yikes. I know I'm a sinner. And this clearly says that the wage (payment, or penalty) of my sin is death. Thankfully, that's not the end of that verse. "For the wages of sin is death, **but** the gift of God is eternal life in Christ Jesus our Lord." Thank God for that beautiful *but*. I deserve death because of my sin, but the gift of God is eternal life because of Jesus.

Here's another one from Ephesians 2:

As for you, you were dead in your transgressions and sins, in which you used to live when you followed the ways of this world and of the ruler of the kingdom of the air, the spirit who is now at work in those who are disobedient. All of us also lived among them at one time, gratifying the cravings of our flesh and following its desires and thoughts. Like the rest, we were by nature deserving of wrath.

—Eph. 2:1–3

Sounds pretty awful, doesn't it? Enter another beautiful but:

But because of his great love for us, God, who is rich in mercy, made us alive with Christ even when we were dead in transgressions—it is by grace you have been saved.

—Eph. 2:4–5

Some people think God isn't fair. Do you really want Him to be? If He was fair, I wouldn't have eternal life. I wouldn't be saved. I would only be known as a sinner who had no part in the Kingdom. But . . . His grace tells another story.

God isn't fair. And I'm so thankful for that. Signed, a sinner saved by grace.

Chapter Eighteen

People

This is a story that I'm not proud of, but it was a huge moment in my life and a very teachable moment now. I always want to be open and honest about my shortcomings and how God has used me through those, and I encourage you to do the same in your life. If we share stories from our weakness, we'll never run out of material.

I lived in Indianapolis for a while with one of my friends from college who happened to be a different nationality than I am. We became close friends, and I was excited when things worked out to room together. We went to get some groceries one night, and as we were leaving, I saw a group of people that were the same nationality as my friend. I've never had thoughts in my life of discrimination, or thinking I'm better than people of other nationalities, or hating them or anything like that. But I was young and naive at this time, and the temptation was sometimes there to make jokes about people who were different from me. I know I'm not alone in having that temptation, because so many of us don't always know how to deal with people who are different from us. And in that moment, I was tempted to make a joke about this group of people, and I had to stop myself because I realized: "Wow . . . my roommate is the same as that group of people, and I almost made a joke about them." My friend would have laughed it off if I had said anything, but that wasn't the point.

Here's what happened: Because he was my friend, because I was close to him, and because I knew him personally, I no longer saw him as a different nationality. I saw him as my friend. I saw him as my brother. And I will never forget that night. God taught me something extremely valuable: we need to see everybody as He sees them. When we get to know people and view them as our brothers and sisters, it changes everything. I want to see all people as children of God. Searching for seven includes seeing Jesus in everybody we meet.

We all need a little *Remember the Titans* in our lives: when the nurse tells Gary that Julius isn't allowed in the room because he's not family, Gary says: "Alice, are you blind? Don't you see the family resemblance? That's my brother."[1]

I love when God sends a wake-up call. It sounds strange, but I want to feel conviction from God in my life. That's another negative-sounding word, but such an important word if I'm really searching for seven. Thank God that He used one of my mistakes to teach me a valuable lesson for my future. When we start to see each person as a child of God, our perspective changes. It gives us the opportunity to reach out and love those who are different from us. "Man looks on the outward appearance, but the LORD looks on the heart" (1 Sam. 16:7 ESV).

I've heard many teachers say, "I've never liked a kid less when I've gotten to know them more." That's a beautiful truth. Statistics show that when you get to know someone you disagree with, you tend to feel differently about that person or who they represent. We need to spend more time getting to really know people, and we need to see the good in people instead of always picking out the bad. Sometimes, I'll watch a TV show, and think, "Why did they drive to their house to say that? They could've just called or sent a quick text." This is one thing TV shows get right about life. If we take some time and invest in real relationships with people, the better off we'll be.

We need people in our lives who believe in us, and we need to be that person for others. When I was a kid, I remember not wanting to put my seatbelt on. My mom would look at me and then take her seatbelt off. I would ask, "What are you doing?" And she would say: "If you're going to die in an accident, so am I." She did that so I would feel guilty and put my seatbelt on. But I also think she was serious. I remembered that example my entire life. It was her way of showing me: "I care about you, and I will always support and protect you in this life." We need people to be there for us and with us. We were never meant to do life alone.

Here's another truth when it comes to the people in our lives: they've been put there by God for a reason. When we know someone personally, it's easier to overlook what they're capable of and what they can teach us. We tend to glamorize people we don't know. We listen to what the celebrity pastor says, even though our own pastor has been teaching the same thing for years. We downplay some of our friends' accomplishments because we've known them our whole lives and act like it's a fluke or not that big of a deal. Ask yourself: Am I taking my pastors, teachers, coaches, parents, or friends for granted? Or do I see the value they bring to my life, and do I believe they're in my life for a reason?

I sometimes get asked to be a guest speaker at camps, FCA events, or things of that nature. When you're a guest speaker, you sometimes get different treatment than you get in your own church. One of my youth group kids was asked by someone at a camp, "Wow, you actually know that guy?!" I'm at a camp, and I have a stage and a microphone, so I must be really important right? But I guarantee some of my own youth groups have thought, "Another message from Tyler tonight. Big deal." I'm guilty of this too, and I don't want to be. Every time my pastor preaches, I know God can teach me something through it. Even if I've heard the speaker a thousand times. When my parents give me advice, I don't want to downplay it just because they're my parents. When my friend does something great in life, I want to celebrate with them. We've got to stop overlooking who God has put in our life. They can teach us amazing things if we just pay attention.

My biggest faith transformation took place in college, and it was because of the people. I learned a lot from the classes and the professors, but it was the late-night dorm room talks that made the biggest impression on me. It was the random discussions about life and theology with my brothers and sisters in Christ that started to shape my faith and who I was becoming. What about you? Do you have those kinds of conversations? Are you ever the one to start those conversations? Surround yourself with people who can help shape your faith; be that person for others.

Bob Goff says, "When we're looking for a plan, God often sends us a person."[2] People come and go in our lives, but many of them have specific roles to play in our story. Give a listening ear to the people you trust. Don't overlook who God has put right in front of you. When we're searching for God, He will often send a person to us with a message.

Compassion

To see people as children of God, we need to learn what compassion truly means. Biblically, it comes from the Greek verb *splagchnizomai*. This word doesn't mean to have a little pity or feel sorry for somebody else. It means being so moved by what they're going through that it causes you to hurt for them. When Scripture says "Jesus had compassion" on somebody, it means He was hurting for them and their situation.

When Jesus landed and saw a large crowd, he had compassion on them, because they were like sheep without a shepherd.

—Mark 6:34

Jesus had compassion on them and healed their sick.

—Matt. 14:14

Jesus had compassion on them and touched their eyes. Immediately they received their sight.

—Matt. 20:34

Moved with compassion, Jesus reached out and touched him. "I am willing," he said. "Be healed!"

—Mark 1:41 NLT

I want to feel compassion for the homeless person on the street corner instead of assuming anything about their life. I want to feel compassion for the single mom who's having a hard time. I want to feel compassion for the atheist who's bashing my faith. I don't know what they've been through. And I want to be aware of opportunities all around me to show this compassion.

Most of the amazing things Jesus did in His ministry were done while He was in public, with people, at random times. He would be passing through a town, on His way to somewhere else, when the needs of others would arise. There were definitely times when He preached sermons and taught in the synagogues, but a huge portion of His ministry was simply being among the people—not from planned events, but from opportunities that presented themselves randomly. There is a great need for listening to sermons. There is a great need for missions work. There's a great need for service projects. But let's also never forget that sometimes, the best opportunities to show compassion will come at unexpected and unplanned times— with your friends, when you're at work, when you're at school, etc. We can't ever forget Jesus's ministry was never confined to a building and was never confined to only listening to others teach.

Erwin McManus said, "It's not about going to church. It's about being the church. The building doesn't need us. . . . Humanity does."[3]

There are needs all around us, and we've got to listen to the prompting of the Holy Spirit and what the Spirit is calling us to do. To have the kind of compassion Jesus had, we need to see the people around us as His children.

I'll never forget a story I heard a pastor share nearly 20 years ago. A long time ago in a poverty-stricken country, there was a little boy, about six years old who was walking on the street. There was a vehicle speeding out of control, and it struck the boy and then kept on driving away. The boy looked lifeless, as many people from the village were watching with horror in their eyes. Just then, there was a lady screaming and running toward the child, so everybody assumed it was the boy's mother. But when she got to the boy, she picked him up to see if it was her son, and after picking him up, she dropped him to the ground, smiled, and told everyone watching: "It's okay, everyone! It's not mine!" And she went away, leaving the boy on the ground.

That's heartbreaking. Whether someone is hurt or not, we cannot ignore the needs of others, as if it's not our problem. Every child is a child of God. Every grown person is a child of God. When we think serving others just isn't our problem, we fail to have the compassion that Jesus modeled in His life. Whatever we do to the least of these, we do unto Christ.

"Therefore, as God's chosen people, holy and dearly loved, clothe yourselves with compassion, kindness, humility, gentleness and patience" (Col. 3:12). Think of compassion like putting your clothes on. We need to put on compassion like it's something we should wear every day.

Unlike our clothes, compassion will never go out of style.

Chapter Nineteen
Story Time

I still remember proposing to my wife like it was yesterday. Boys, take some notes if you'd like to steal my idea. My girlfriend had always wanted me to sing to her, but I never had enough courage to do it. I figured it was time. I didn't sing just any song to her, however. I wanted something from the heart. About 10 years prior, I had written a song called "Can't Wait," and it was a song about my future wife that I hadn't met yet. I only had lyrics and no music, so I had a buddy of mine write a guitar part that I could use for the song. We had a youth group event that night, and when it was over, I asked her if she wanted to go walk on a trail that we had been to a few times. When we got there, I said, "It's fun to listen to music out here, so I brought this portable music player." What she didn't know was I had the song queued up and ready to go. I sang her the song, and thankfully, nobody walked by at that time. Can you imagine singing a song to your girlfriend and somebody walks by with their pit bull?

After singing her the world premiere of "Can't Wait," I told her I loved her for the first time and asked her to be my wife. For some reason, she said yes, and we were engaged. The first thing we wanted to do after getting engaged was to tell the world about our news. That's how it should be. Good news is meant to be shared, right? We called her sister, then my sister. We drove to her parents' house, then my parents' house. We then posted it on social media and continued to call and text people throughout the night.

Here's my question: What if that's not how the story went? What if she responded by saying, "Yes, I will marry you. But we can't tell anybody about it." I would have thought, "What do you mean we can't tell anybody? We have this amazing news. Why wouldn't we want to share it with the world?"

Here's the thing. We do this all the time to our bridegroom. Jesus is the groom, and His Church is the bride. And even though we are the bride of Christ and we have the best news in the world to share, we often keep it to ourselves. We make up excuses constantly as to why we don't proclaim this news like we should. We'd rather share about news in the sports world, or a big promotion we got, or other personal achievements. There's nothing wrong with sharing those things, but at what point does sharing about Jesus become the most important thing?

I've noticed that Christians love to say this famous line: "Preach the gospel and when necessary, use words." Yes, actions can speak louder than words, and your words won't mean jack if your life and example don't match up. But too many Christians use this quote as an excuse so they never have to actually talk about their faith. If we're really going to reach people, we'll have to actually open our mouths from time to time and share. As it says in Romans 10:14, "How, then, can they call on the one they have not believed in? And how can they believe in the one of whom they have not heard? And how can they hear without someone preaching to them?"

I remember hanging out in St. Augustine, Florida, one afternoon when I lived in the area. I was on a busy street that a lot of tourists liked to visit. There was a large group of people carrying signs claiming the world was going to end the next day. They were out there to "warn us" about God's judgment. Apparently, these "Christians" had never read Matthew 24:36, or maybe they thought they were smarter than Jesus Himself. The world obviously did not end the next day or any other day that's been predicted to this point. But I remember having this thought: The world *will* end tomorrow for about 154,000 people. That's the average number of worldwide deaths per day. That's a big number. And even if Jesus doesn't come back for another 10,000 years, our lives will end much sooner than that. We have the best news in the world to share, but only a short time to share it. It's time we find the sense of urgency needed for this life-changing message.

The best way to share about God's story is to share your story, but let God be the main character. It should never be about what I've done but what God has done through me. When people look at your story, what will they see? Nobody will ever know your entire story, but they'll see parts of it. And every part is just as important as the rest.

Imagine that your life story is written out on paper—thousands and thousands of words written down, in order. Think about that person who you only see in that one class you share, or that person you only see once a week at church, or that person you only got to work with for a few years. That person is only reading a small portion of your story. What are they reading? Think about that coworker or that teammate who may see a little more of your story. Do they see a story that reflects God?

And let's make one thing very clear: there is no such thing as a "boring testimony." To be honest, I hope my kids claim to have one of those. If they don't have to do drugs or have a conversion in prison, I'll be more than okay with that. But no matter what our conversion stories look like, each one is special and amazing. No one else has the story that you have. If you were dead in your sin, on a path toward hell, and Jesus saved you and gave you a future, there's nothing boring about that.

We all need to share our story. There's power in our words. Proverbs 18:21 says, "The tongue has the power of life and death." Most people want to make a difference, but they feel too small or insignificant to really do anything. But this verse says that our words have the power to bring life to someone or death to someone. That's a big deal. What you say to someone in a time of need could change the trajectory of their life. You don't need a stage or huge audience to make a difference. Speak life to the person sitting across from you. If your words have that much power, use them wisely. Shout about your God from the rooftops. Bring encouragement. And never stop.

You don't need a Bible degree to share your story. You don't need to work at a church. You don't even need to have a bunch of knowledge about the Bible. Brand-new Christians should proclaim everything Jesus has done in their life. Look at the blind man that was healed in John 9. After he was healed, the people were questioning him about Jesus. The man said, "Whether he is a sinner or not, I don't know. One thing I do know. I was blind but now I see" (John 9:25). Couldn't we all have that mindset when it comes to sharing about Jesus? I don't have all the answers, but one thing I know for sure: I was blind, and now I can see. I was in darkness, but now I'm in light. I was on a path toward hell, but now He's saved me for all eternity. Share what you do know, and don't hold back.

Sometimes, we don't share about Jesus because we're afraid of what others will think. Will I lose friends? Will I be made fun of? What if they humiliate me with questions I don't know how to answer? Here's the cold-hard truth: if we are never getting made fun of for our faith and if we're never losing friendships because of our faith, it probably means we aren't doing enough. Scripture says we will be persecuted and mocked and that the world will hate us because of Jesus. These things are more severe in certain parts of the world. But if these things are never happening to us, even on a smaller level, we need to take a look in the mirror and realize we aren't talking about Jesus enough. I don't enjoy it when others make fun of me, and I don't enjoy it when others hate me. But nothing brings me a greater joy than living out the gospel. If I'm truly living my faith out, these things will happen. The more I share about Jesus, the more chances there will be to get mocked and hated.

We all want to hear positive things from others in our story. We all want validation. We want to be liked and appreciated. Unfortunately, we won't always hear those things, even when we deserve to. Despite having thousands of fans along with lots of critics, Jon Foreman says, "I'm really only responsible to make sure One person is clapping at the end of my life."[1] As much as I want to hear "Good job," or "You're awesome," or "Thank you" in my life, there are two words I would much rather hear. I long for the day when my Maker looks me squarely in the eye and says, "Well done." Those words will be worth every second of pain I've ever faced. Those words will be the ultimate end (and beginning) to my story. And when I leave this earth and hear those words, I may be speechless. But if I'm able to speak in that moment, I will say these words: "I've been searching for You every day of my life, and now I'm home."

Searching for Seven:
Discussion Questions

Chapter One: The Search Begins

1. Has God ever used something in your life to lead to something else later on? What did you learn along the way?

2. "It's hard to find what we're not actively searching for." Instead of just hoping for God to "show up," are you actively searching for Him? In what ways?

3. Read through the parable of the workers in the vineyard (Matthew 20:1–16). What group would you fall into at this point in your life? What do you think Jesus is teaching us about the 11th hour workers?

4. When we've screwed up, God doesn't just leave us on the bench. He puts us right back in the game. What is God calling you to do this week to get back in?

Chapter Two: When in Doubt, Serve

1. What items in your house have quit working because you haven't used them?

2. Read multiple translations of Ephesians 2:10. What does it mean to be "created in Christ to do good works"?

3. Could serving others actually help with serious issues such as depression, suicidal thoughts, marital problems, and self-worth? Discuss.

4. Read and meditate on 1 Corinthians 15:58. What does this verse mean to you? Does it give you motivation to serve regardless of how others respond?

Chapter Three: Faith

1. What's the difference between faith and hope? What's the difference between a blind faith and a faith that is "sure and certain"?

2. Who are some of your favorite Christian apologists to follow? Download the Cross-Examined app and look through some of the questions and answers to faith-related topics. Researching the evidence will help our faith grow beyond a blind belief. (Look up Frank Turek, Ravi Zacharias, Sean McDowell, the late Nabeel Qureshi, William Lane Craig, Lee Strobel, and J. Warner Wallace for great resources.)

3. Read through Hebrews 11 and discuss the action that each hero of our faith took. What does faith in action look like for you?

4. What evidence do we have that Christianity is real?

Chapter Four: Just Say Yes

1. Have you ever said no to something faith-related and regretted it? Name a time when you said yes and describe what happened through your experience.

2. Have you ever felt like Moses? Could God be telling you, "I know you can do this. I'm the One who made you"?

3. Name a time you spent a lot of money on an experience. Was it worth it? How can we "experience" our faith each day?

4. How can we truly live out our faith seven days a week?

Chapter Five: It's Alive!

1. Have you ever met a celebrity? What happened? What's the difference between knowing of God and really knowing God?

2. Can you think of a time when a Bible verse or story came alive for you? What happened, and how did God speak to you through His Word?

3. Plenty of people know Scripture (including the Pharisees and Satan), but they take it out of context. How can we make sure we're not just reading it but being transformed by it?

4. Read through the story in Matthew 12. Why do you think Jesus told them to remember the story of Jonah when they asked for a miracle? Do we treat God's Word like a miracle every day?

Chapter Six: Illusions

1. What's the biggest lie you ever told as a kid? Play "two truths and a lie" and see who can fool the rest of the group!

2. What are the biggest lies the powers of darkness want us to believe? For each lie, try to find a Scripture that is God's response to that illusion.

3. Have you ever struggled with your identity? How can we live so that our identity isn't found in our greatest accomplishments, our biggest failures, or even what we're known for?

4. Look through Ecclesiastes. What can Solomon's words from years ago teach us about illusions and truth today?

Chapter Seven: Platforms and Talents

1. What platforms do you have right now? Which ones are you using, and which ones could you be using more for the Kingdom?

2. Read the parable of the talents (Matthew 25:14–30). What can this story teach us?

3. Has God used you more through your talents or your weaknesses? Explain.

4. What does it mean to be salt and light?

Chapter Eight: Choose the Right Battles

1. Which battles should Christians be fighting and not fighting in the world today? What is most important?

2. Is it possible to be a "peacemaker" in this political climate? Do you agree with Timothy Keller that the first Christians wouldn't have been fully Republican or Democrat?

3. Christians should hold one another accountable, confront sin, and learn to "disagree in a loving way." How can we do this? What has worked/not worked for you?

4. Paul said we have a "ministry of reconciliation." What does that mean? What needs to be reconciled right now in your family, neighborhood, workplace, or church?

Chapter Nine: Seven Times Seventy Times

1. Read the powerful story of Eric Smallridge and forgiveness here at https://www.christianpost.com/news/mother-does-the-impossible-forgives-drunk-driver-who-killed-her-daughter-gets-him-out-of-prison-early-video.html What are your thoughts?

2. Aside from Jesus Himself, what's the most powerful story of forgiveness you've ever heard?

3. What does the "seven times seventy times" phrase mean in your life? Who do you need to forgive?

4. The second you come to Christ is the second you are forgiven. What Bible stories back that up?

Chapter Ten: Contentment

1. "If God is your shepherd, why are you still in want?" What is an area of your life where contentment is needed?

2. Read through the blind man's story in John 9. When might this story be a great testimony to share with someone? In your own life, have you ever used bad circumstances to show God's power?

3. Matthew 13:44 says, "The kingdom of heaven is like treasure hidden in a field. When a man found it, he hid it again, and then in his joy went and sold all he had, and bought that field." Do we live our lives this way?

4. What are some of your best days spent on this planet? Share some stories. Now combine all of them: they won't equal even one day in heaven!

Chapter Eleven: Confidence and Comparison

1. Have you ever felt like the characters in *The Wizard of Oz* when approaching God? Have you ever felt like the singers on *The Voice* hoping to do well enough for God to turn around? How does Hebrews 4:16 change that mindset?

2. What role does comparison play when it comes to contentment and confidence in who we are in Christ? How can we fight back against the comparison game?

3. What area of your life are you most confident in? What area needs some work in that department? Most importantly, how can we live our lives being confident of our identity as a child of God?

4. Read Luke 18:9–14. Which person are you, and why?

Chapter Twelve: Faith Like a Child

1. What's the difference between a childish faith and a childlike faith?

2. Asking questions is a good thing. Write down a few questions that you have about God, Christianity, or the Bible. Put them in a pile and select a few to discuss over the next few weeks.

3. Like the parable of the wedding banquet, how can you take the lowest seat today? What does that look like in different situations of your life?

4. To have faith like a child, we should never stop asking questions and never stop dreaming. What is a dream of yours that you've always thought about but never tried? Is today the day to start chasing it again?

Chapter Thirteen: A Sense of Wonder

1. What's your favorite place you've ever visited, and why? What place makes you feel like a kid in Disneyland? How can we get to that place in our relationship with God?

2. In Romans 1:25, Paul said, "They exchanged the truth about God for a lie, and worshiped and served created things rather than the Creator—who is forever praised." What areas of your life have you been worshipping the created things instead of the Creator Himself?

3. When's the last time you "took off your sandals" and believed you were standing on holy ground? Let's do that right now!

4. Do you have a go-to spot to spend time with God? Jesus would often find a solitary place to spend time with God. Where's your place? If you don't have one, find one this week!

Chapter Fourteen: No Pain, No Gain

1. To the best of your understanding, why do you believe there's so much pain in this world?

2. Look up C. S. Lewis's quote about the crooked and straight line. Lewis was an atheist when he couldn't understand why there was so much pain the world. He became a Christian when he realized pain meant there had to be good as well. How does his quote speak to you?

3. Does pain typically turn you away from God or toward Him? Do you have past examples to share?

4. Read through some of the Psalms, paying attention to how the writers would cry out to God. They were sometimes angry, upset, or confused. Yet they still brought everything before God. What can the Psalms teach us about our relationship with God and the pain we face?

Chapter Fifteen: Will Call

1. What is your career calling, and what is your daily calling as a Christian? What are a few things you know God has called you to do in this life?

2. What does the Bible say when it refers to the words *today* and *tomorrow*?

3. Read back through the Jon Foreman and David Platt quotes from this chapter. What do you think about what they had to say?

4. How do you know what God wants you to do in your life?

Chapter Sixteen: Whatevers and Weirdos

1. Christians should be "weird" but in a good way. As a group, make a list of ways Christians should be weird in a good way or ways they've been notoriously weird in a negative way.

2. Read Colossians 3:23 and Philippians 4:8–9. How can you apply these verses to your life?

3. Do you believe in aliens? ET? UFOs? Christians are "aliens" in this world, and our citizenship is in heaven. How does that truth impact your life and those around you?

4. How do you "silence the ignorant talk of foolish people" as Scripture says to do?

Chapter Seventeen: Grace vs. Law

1. If God loves us, why does He have so many rules and commands to follow?

2. How would you describe the difference between grace and law? Why is this such an important topic to understand when it comes to Christianity?

3. In the Prodigal Son story, why are verses 17–18 in Luke 15 so overlooked? What do those verses mean for us?

4. Read through Galatians 3 and Romans 7. How different are these Scriptures from the legalistic worldview many people have today about church and faith?

Chapter Eighteen: People

1. Who have been some influential people in your life? What qualities do they have, and how have they impacted you?

2. What people in your life have you taken for granted? Give them a text or phone call and let them know you appreciate them!

3. Jesus had compassion on the people who were hurting and broken. What would help us to see people as His children even if they're different from us?

4. How might we "clothe ourselves with compassion" each day?

Chapter Nineteen: Story Time

1. Share the short version of your testimony. It's one of the greatest things you can ever share in your life!

2. What stops us from sharing about Jesus with the world? How can we get over those fears or excuses?

3. What is the best compliment you've ever received? How will that compare to hearing "well done" from your Maker one day?

4. Though this study ends, the search is just beginning. How will you actively search for God in the coming days, weeks, months, and years? Let's help one another as we "seek first His righteousness."

Notes

Chapter Two: When in Doubt, Serve

1. Francis Chan, *You and Me Forever: Marriage in Light of Eternity* (San Francisco: Claire Love Publishing, 2014), 7.
2. Martin Luther King Jr., https://www.goodreads.com/ quotes/757-everybody-can -be-great-because-anybody-can-serve-you-don-t-have.

Chapter Five: It's Alive!

1. C. S. Lewis, *Prince Caspian: The Return to Narnia, The Chronicles of Narnia* (New York: Harper Collins, 1951), 141.
2. C. S. Lewis, *Mere Christianity* (London: Geoffrey Bles, 1952), 141.
3. "Leadership Quotes from Spurgeon," https://leadership.lifeway.com/2016/04/11 /leadership-quotes-from-charles-spurgeon-part-two/.
4. A. W. Tozer, *The Pursuit of God, Illustrated Edition* (SWB Books, 1948).

Chapter Seven: Platforms and Talents

1. Lecrae Moore, *Unashamed* (Nashville, TN: B & H Publishing Group, 2006), 30.

Chapter Eight: Choose the Right Battles

1. Bob Goff (@bobgoff), "It will be our love, not our opinions which will be our greatest contribution to the world." Twitter, March 22, 2014, 8:50 a.m., https:// twitter.com/bobgoff/status/447399893628620800.
2. Bob Goff, *Everybody, Always: Becoming Love in a World Full of Setbacks and Difficult People* (Nashville, TN: Nelson Books, 2018), 11.
3. Andy Stanley (@andystanley), "Most bad church experiences are the result of somebody prioritizing a VIEW over a YOU, something Jesus never did and instructed us not to do either," Twitter, August 31, 2018, 11:30 a.m., https:// twitter.com/AndyStanley/status/1035595643241291778.

4. Timothy Keller, "How Do Christians Fit Into the Two-Party System? They Don't" *New York Times*, September 29, 2018, https://www.nytimes.com/2018/09/29/opinion/sunday/christians-politics-belief.html.

Chapter Nine: Seven Times Seventy Times

1. Steve Hartman, "Mother's Forgiveness Gives Convict Second Chance," CBS News, November 30, 2012, https://www.cbsnews.com/news/mothers-forgiveness-gives-convict-second-chance/.

Chapter Ten: Contentment

1. C. S. Lewis, *Mere Christianity* (London: Geoffrey Bles, 1952), 32.
2. Charles Spurgeon, *Commentary on the New Testament* (New Zealand: Titus Books, 1917), 146.

Chapter Eleven: Confidence and Comparison

1. Thomas Watson, "The Christian Soldier," https://www.fivesolas.com/Watson/soldie_i.htm.
2. Steven Furtick (@stevenfurtick), "One reason we struggle w/insecurity: we're comparing our behind the scenes to everyone else's highlight reel," Twitter, May 10, 2011, 8:58 a.m., https://twitter.com/stevenfurtick/status/67981913746444288.
3. Mike Donehey (@mikedonehey), "What would it be like, if the people of God didn't care who God used, as long as He moved? I think rivers of joy would open before us," Twitter, December 31, 2015, 11:41 a.m., https://twitter.com/mikedonehey/status/682647858382811136.
4. Donehey, (@mikedonehey), "Imagine if we didn't even need to be used by God? What if we were just as stoked when God used someone else?" Twitter, December 11, 2015, 12:58 p.m., https://twitter.com/mikedonehey/status/675419437969862658.
5. Crag Groeschel (@craiggroeschel), "Comparison will either make you feel superior or inferior. Neither honors God," Twitter, June 18, 2019, 10:00 p.m., https://twitter.com/craiggroeschel/status/1141209007367098369.

Chapter Twelve: Faith Like a Child

1. C. S. Lewis, *Mere Christianity,* chap. 8, "The Great Sin," Kindle edition.

Chapter Thirteen: A Sense of Wonder

1. Abraham Joshua Heschel, *The Ragamuffin Gospel* (Colorado Springs, CO: Multnomah Books, 2000), 34.

2. A. W. Tozer, *The Pursuit of God* (Camp Hill, PA: Wing Spread Publishers, 1982), 59.
3. Tozer, *Pursuit of God*, 89.
4. Tozer, "Tragedy: Men Do Not Know That God Is Here," *Words of Hope*, June 2, 1999, https://www.woh.org/devotional/1999/06/02/tragedy-men-do-not-know-that-god-is-here/.
5. Ravi Zacharias, *Recapture the Wonder: Experiencing God's Amazing Promise of Childlike Joy* (Nashville, TN: Integrity Publishers, 2003), 51.
6. D. S. Martin, "Mary Oliver: Pay Attention, Be Astonished, Talk About It," *Ruminate*, September 01, 2008, https://www.ruminatemagazine.com/blogs /ruminate-blog/mary-oliver-pay-attention-be-astonished-talk-about-it.

Chapter Fourteen: No Pain, No Gain

1. "The Little Girl Who Doesn't Feel Pain," *The Oprah Winfrey Show* (November 8, 2005), https://www.oprah.com/own-oprahshow/watch-an-oprah-show -guest-gabby-gingras-who-feels-no-pain-video.
2. Bart Millard, *I Can Only Imagine—Small Group Kit* (City on a Hill: 2018), DVD.
3. "R. C. Sproul Quotes and Sayings," *inspiringquotes.us,* https://www.inspiring quotes.us/author/8501-r-c-sproul.
4. Zig Ziglar, "No Elevator to Success," https://www.ziglar.com/quotes/success -and-failure.
5. Bethany Hamilton, *Soul Surfer,* https://bethanyhamilton.com/%E2%80%8Bi -dont-need-easy/.
6. Jon Foreman, "Switchfoot: Oh? Gravity. The Meaning Behind," *Christianity Today* (December 2006), https://www.christiantoday.com/article/switchfoot.oh.gravity .the.meaning.behind/8828.htm.

Chapter Fifteen: Will Call

1. Chandler Vannoy, "What We Get Wrong about 'Finding God's Will,'" *Relevant* magazine (September 2019), https://relevantmagazine.com/god /what-we-get-wrong-about-finding-gods-will/.
2. "Choosing to Believe with Jon Foreman," Unsigned interview in *Relevant* magazine (March 2014), https://relevantmagazine.com/culture /choosing-believe-jon-foreman/.
3. Martin Luther, https://www.goodreads.com/ quotes/203914-there-are-two-days -in-my-calendar-this-day-and.
4. David Platt, *Radical* (Colorado Springs, CO: Multnomah Books, 2010), 159.
5. "Walt Disney Company Quotes," https://www.goodreads.com/quotes /9425979-we-don-t-make-movies-to-make-money-we-make-money.

6. Moore, *Unashamed*, 65.
7. Rich Mullins, https://lightraiders.com/fighting-giants/.

Chapter Sixteen: Whatevers and Weirdos

1. A. W. Tozer (@TozerAW), "Go to church once a week and nobody pays attention. Worship God seven days a week and you become strange," Twitter, September 3, 2015, 9:07 a.m., https://twitter.com/tozeraw/status/639469794928955392.

Chapter Seventeen: Grace vs. Law

1. Charles Spurgeon, "The Great Physician and His Patients," March 1864, Metropolitan Tabernacle Pulpit, https://www.spurgeon.org/resource-library /sermons/the-great-physician-and-his-patients#flipbook/.
2. Tim Keller, *AZ Quotes.com*, https://www.azquotes.com/quote/935476.

Chapter Eighteen: People

1. *Remember the Titans*, Directed by Boaz Yakin. Burbank, CA: Walt Disney Pictures, 2000.
2. Bob Goff, *Everybody Always*, 91.
3. Erwin McManus, sermon, November 2014, https://vimeo.com/112036988.

Chapter Nineteen: Story Time

1. "Jon Foreman Quotes and Sayings," *Inspiring Quotes,* https://www.inspiring quotes.us/author/5974-jon-foreman/page:2.

Tyler Would Love to Hear from You!

You can find Tyler on twitter at @TylerSmith_ISL and @tysmitty21. Send him a text at 765-365-4838, or find him online at tylerdsmith.net. Search "Alektor" on downloadyouthministry.com for a three-week DVD resource.

9 781939 815606